POWERSHELL AND GET-CIMINSTANCE

When one is not enough!

Richard Thomas Edwards

CONTENTS

Okay, let's get this show on the road

As I write this my wife and I were watching the advertorials on just how great the RV lifestyle is. Two immediate thoughts come to mind. If you have to have a show on how great the lifestyle is, you don't need a show. Second, why not have a balanced point of view? Well, they told me but as I soon discovered.... You get the picture.

But then I realized something else, too. Books – especially, technical ones - are a lot like lifestyle alternatives, too. Funny thing is, most programmers are going to look at the book title, see if it was written by someone they know or published by a brand they made purchases with and never, ever purchase one of mine.

What they don't know is the older generation of programmers who had technical support issues between 1996 and 2002 – or who went up to the newsgroups between 2002 and 2005 most likely talked to me or read one of my newsgroup threads. I did 3,000 cases and 3,000 newsgroup articles back then. And I worked at Microsoft from 1996 to 2002.

I would have worked longer at Microsoft, but they outsourced our technical support jobs.

Yep. You've never heard of me.

Hopefully, you will get something out of this "no name" through my book.

Enough said about all of that.

So, what is this book about?

It is about Get–CIMInstance, basically, Microsoft's newest PowerShell kid on the block. And while I do embrace this as a replacement for the Get–CIMInstance, I'm not so sure the ramifications of this change is – from a programmer's perspective – a good one. In fact, I'm beginning to wonder if PowerShell isn't Microsoft's way of telling a lot of programmers to go away.

But that is my point of view. You will have yours. I just don't think VBScript, JScript, Kixtart, Perl script, Python, Rexx or Ruby should be shelved because Microsoft's mighty PowerShell does it better.

Perhaps, true from an Administrator's point of view. But from a programmer's perspective, all scripting languages deserve the right to be out there and working with Windows, too.

So why does Get-CIMInstance tell me it is not a programmers' solution?

Up until now, you would get this:

```
instance of Win32_Process
{
    Caption = "System Idle Process";
    CreationClassName = "Win32_Process";
    CSCreationClassName = "Win32_ComputerSystem";
    CSName = "WIN-VNQ7KUKQ4NE";
    Description = "System Idle Process";
    Handle = "0";
    HandleCount = 0;
    KernelModeTime = "5138396562500";
    Name = "System Idle Process";
    OSCreationClassName = "Win32_OperatingSystem";
    OSName    =    "Microsoft    Windows    Server    2012    R2    Standard
Evaluation|C:\\Windows|\\Device\\Harddisk1\\Partition2";
    OtherOperationCount = "0";
    OtherTransferCount = "0";
    PageFaults = 1;
    PageFileUsage = 0;
    ParentProcessId = 0;
    PeakPageFileUsage = 0;
    PeakVirtualSize = "65536";
    PeakWorkingSetSize = 24;
    Priority = 0;
    PrivatePageCount = "0";
    ProcessId = 0;
    QuotaNonPagedPoolUsage = 0;
    QuotaPagedPoolUsage = 0;
```

```
        QuotaPeakNonPagedPoolUsage = 0;
        QuotaPeakPagedPoolUsage = 0;
        ReadOperationCount = "0";
        ReadTransferCount = "0";
        SessionId = 0;
        ThreadCount = 8;
        UserModeTime = "0";
        VirtualSize = "65536";
        WindowsVersion = "6.3.9600";
        WorkingSetSize = "24576";
        WriteOperationCount = "0";
        WriteTransferCount = "0";
    };
```

With Get-CIMInstance, you get this:

That's right, absolutely nothing. But when I type $obj | Get-Member, I get:

```
  Caption                    Property        string Caption {get;}
  CommandLine                Property        string CommandLine {get;}
  CreationClassName           Property        string CreationClassName
{get;}
  CreationDate                  Property         CimInstance#DateTime
CreationDate {get;}
  CSCreationClassName        Property        string CSCreationClassName
{get;}
  CSName                     Property        string CSName {get;}
  Description                Property        string Description {get;}
  ExecutablePath               Property          string ExecutablePath
{get;}
  ExecutionState               Property          uint16 ExecutionState
{get;}
  Handle                     Property        string Handle {get;}
  HandleCount                Property        uint32 HandleCount {get;}
  InstallDate                  Property          CimInstance#DateTime
InstallDate {get;}
  KernelModeTime               Property          uint64 KernelModeTime
{get;}
```

```
   MaximumWorkingSetSize                    Property                  uint32
MaximumWorkingSetSize {get;}
   MinimumWorkingSetSize                    Property                  uint32
MinimumWorkingSetSize {get;}
   Name                      Property       string Name {get;}
   OSCreationClassName       Property       string OSCreationClassName
{get;}
   OSName                    Property       string OSName {get;}
   OtherOperationCount       Property       uint64 OtherOperationCount
{get;}
   OtherTransferCount        Property       uint64 OtherTransferCount
{get;}
   PageFaults                Property       uint32 PageFaults {get;}
   PageFileUsage                  Property         uint32 PageFileUsage
{get;}
   ParentProcessId             Property         uint32 ParentProcessId
{get;}
   PeakPageFileUsage          Property        uint32 PeakPageFileUsage
{get;}
   PeakVirtualSize             Property          uint64 PeakVirtualSize
{get;}
   PeakWorkingSetSize         Property        uint32 PeakWorkingSetSize
{get;}
   Priority                  Property       uint32 Priority {get;}
   PrivatePageCount           Property        uint64 PrivatePageCount
{get;}
   ProcessId                 Property       uint32 ProcessId {get;}
   PSComputerName              Property         string PSComputerName
{get;}
   QuotaNonPagedPoolUsage             Property                  uint32
QuotaNonPagedPoolUsage {get;}
   QuotaPagedPoolUsage       Property       uint32 QuotaPagedPoolUsage
{get;}
   QuotaPeakNonPagedPoolUsage   Property                       uint32
QuotaPeakNonPagedPoolUsage {get;}
   QuotaPeakPagedPoolUsage          Property                   uint32
QuotaPeakPagedPoolUsage {get;}
   ReadOperationCount          Property       uint64 ReadOperationCount
{get;}
   ReadTransferCount         Property        uint64 ReadTransferCount
{get;}
   SessionId                 Property       uint32 SessionId {get;}
   Status                    Property       string Status {get;}
```

```
TerminationDate                    Property          CimInstance#DateTime
TerminationDate {get;}
ThreadCount              Property      uint32 ThreadCount {get;}
UserModeTime             Property      uint64 UserModeTime {get;}
VirtualSize              Property      uint64 VirtualSize {get;}
WindowsVersion            Property       string WindowsVersion
{get;}
WorkingSetSize            Property       uint64 WorkingSetSize
{get;}
WriteOperationCount      Property      uint64 WriteOperationCount
{get;}
WriteTransferCount        Property       uint64 WriteTransferCount
{get;}
Path                          ScriptProperty System.Object Path
{get=$this.ExecutablePath;}
```

Well, as I have already created a program that would create :

```
function generate-information
{
    param
    (
        [Parameter(Mandatory=$True)]
        [string]$MachineName,
        [Parameter(Mandatory=$True)]
        [string]$Namespace,
        [Parameter(Mandatory=$True)]
        [string]$Classname
    )

    $objs = Get-CIMInstance -namespace $Namespace -class $Classname
    if(!($objs.Count))
    {
        write-host "Caption                        : "$objs.Caption
        write-host  "CommandLine                          :
"$objs.CommandLine
        write-host   "CreationClassName                     :
"$objs.CreationClassName
        write-host   "CreationDate                          :
"$objs.CreationDate
        write-host   "CSCreationClassName                   :
"$objs.CSCreationClassName
```

```
        write-host "CSName                    : "$objs.CSName
        write-host  "Description                            :
"$objs.Description
        write-host  "ExecutablePath                         :
"$objs.ExecutablePath
        write-host  "ExecutionState                         :
"$objs.ExecutionState
        write-host "Handle                    : "$objs.Handle
        write-host  "HandleCount                            :
"$objs.HandleCount
        write-host  "InstallDate                            :
"$objs.InstallDate
        write-host  "KernelModeTime                         :
"$objs.KernelModeTime
        write-host   "MaximumWorkingSetSize                 :
"$objs.MaximumWorkingSetSize
        write-host   "MinimumWorkingSetSize                 :
"$objs.MinimumWorkingSetSize
        write-host "Name                      : "$objs.Name
        write-host  "OSCreationClassName                    :
"$objs.OSCreationClassName
        write-host "OSName                    : "$objs.OSName
        write-host  "OtherOperationCount                    :
"$objs.OtherOperationCount
        write-host  "OtherTransferCount                     :
"$objs.OtherTransferCount
        write-host "PageFaults             : "$objs.PageFaults
        write-host  "PageFileUsage                          :
"$objs.PageFileUsage
        write-host  "ParentProcessId                        :
"$objs.ParentProcessId
        write-host  "PeakPageFileUsage                      :
"$objs.PeakPageFileUsage
        write-host  "PeakVirtualSize                        :
"$objs.PeakVirtualSize
        write-host  "PeakWorkingSetSize                     :
"$objs.PeakWorkingSetSize
        write-host "Priority               : "$objs.Priority
        write-host  "PrivatePageCount                       :
"$objs.PrivatePageCount
        write-host "ProcessId              : "$objs.ProcessId
        write-host   "QuotaNonPagedPoolUsage                :
"$objs.QuotaNonPagedPoolUsage
```

```
        write-host   "QuotaPagedPoolUsage                          :
"$objs.QuotaPagedPoolUsage
        write-host      "QuotaPeakNonPagedPoolUsage                 :
"$objs.QuotaPeakNonPagedPoolUsage
        write-host    "QuotaPeakPagedPoolUsage                      :
"$objs.QuotaPeakPagedPoolUsage
        write-host   "ReadOperationCount                            :
"$objs.ReadOperationCount
        write-host   "ReadTransferCount                             :
"$objs.ReadTransferCount
        write-host "SessionId                     : "$objs.SessionId
        write-host "Status                     : "$objs.Status
        write-host   "TerminationDate                               :
"$objs.TerminationDate
        write-host   "ThreadCount                                   :
"$objs.ThreadCount
        write-host   "UserModeTime                                  :
"$objs.UserModeTime
        write-host   "VirtualSize                                   :
"$objs.VirtualSize
        write-host   "WindowsVersion                                :
"$objs.WindowsVersion
        write-host   "WorkingSetSize                                :
"$objs.WorkingSetSize
        write-host    "WriteOperationCount                          :
"$objs.WriteOperationCount
        write-host    "WriteTransferCount                           :
"$objs.WriteTransferCount
        write-host
    }
    else
    {
        foreach($obj in $objs)
        {
            write-host "Caption                       : "$obj.Caption
            write-host   "CommandLine                                :
"$obj.CommandLine
            write-host   "CreationClassName                          :
"$obj.CreationClassName
            write-host   "CreationDate                               :
"$obj.CreationDate
            write-host    "CSCreationClassName                       :
"$obj.CSCreationClassName
            write-host "CSName                        : "$obj.CSName
```

```
            write-host  "Description                                :
"$obj.Description
            write-host  "ExecutablePath                             :
"$obj.ExecutablePath
            write-host  "ExecutionState                             :
"$obj.ExecutionState
            write-host "Handle                        : "$obj.Handle
            write-host  "HandleCount                                :
"$obj.HandleCount
            write-host  "InstallDate                                :
"$obj.InstallDate
            write-host  "KernelModeTime                             :
"$obj.KernelModeTime
            write-host  "MaximumWorkingSetSize                      :
"$obj.MaximumWorkingSetSize
            write-host  "MinimumWorkingSetSize                      :
"$obj.MinimumWorkingSetSize
            write-host "Name                          : "$obj.Name
            write-host  "OSCreationClassName                        :
"$obj.OSCreationClassName
            write-host "OSName                        : "$obj.OSName
            write-host  "OtherOperationCount                        :
"$obj.OtherOperationCount
            write-host  "OtherTransferCount                         :
"$obj.OtherTransferCount
            write-host  "PageFaults                                 :
"$obj.PageFaults
            write-host  "PageFileUsage                              :
"$obj.PageFileUsage
            write-host  "ParentProcessId                            :
"$obj.ParentProcessId
            write-host  "PeakPageFileUsage                          :
"$obj.PeakPageFileUsage
            write-host  "PeakVirtualSize                            :
"$obj.PeakVirtualSize
            write-host  "PeakWorkingSetSize                         :
"$obj.PeakWorkingSetSize
            write-host "Priority                      : "$obj.Priority
            write-host  "PrivatePageCount                           :
"$obj.PrivatePageCount
            write-host  "ProcessId                                  :
"$obj.ProcessId
            write-host  "QuotaNonPagedPoolUsage                     :
"$obj.QuotaNonPagedPoolUsage
```

```
            write-host    "QuotaPagedPoolUsage               :
"$obj.QuotaPagedPoolUsage
            write-host      "QuotaPeakNonPagedPoolUsage       :
"$obj.QuotaPeakNonPagedPoolUsage
            write-host    "QuotaPeakPagedPoolUsage            :
"$obj.QuotaPeakPagedPoolUsage
            write-host    "ReadOperationCount                 :
"$obj.ReadOperationCount
            write-host    "ReadTransferCount                  :
"$obj.ReadTransferCount
            write-host  "SessionId                            :
"$obj.SessionId
            write-host "Status                    : "$obj.Status
            write-host    "TerminationDate                    :
"$obj.TerminationDate
            write-host    "ThreadCount                        :
"$obj.ThreadCount
            write-host    "UserModeTime                       :
"$obj.UserModeTime
            write-host    "VirtualSize                        :
"$obj.VirtualSize
            write-host    "WindowsVersion                     :
"$obj.WindowsVersion
            write-host    "WorkingSetSize                     :
"$obj.WorkingSetSize
            write-host    "WriteOperationCount                :
"$obj.WriteOperationCount
            write-host    "WriteTransferCount                 :
"$obj.WriteTransferCount
            write-host
        }
      }
    }
    generate-information "." "root\CIMV2" "Win32_Process"
```

For this reason and the fact that I have had to do what I'm about to show you to dynamically create WMI based ManagementPacks, below is an example of what is needed to get the most out of Get-CIMInstance:

```
    $objs   =   Get-CIMInstance     -Namespace   root\CIMV2   -Class
Win32_NetworkLoginProfile
    if(!$objs.Count)
    {
        $tstr = ""
```

```
        $tstr = $tstr + "AccountExpires                          :" +
$obj.AccountExpires + [System.Environment]::NewLine
        $tstr = $tstr + "AuthorizationFlags                       :" +
$obj.AuthorizationFlags + [System.Environment]::NewLine
        $tstr = $tstr + "BadPasswordCount                         :" +
$obj.BadPasswordCount + [System.Environment]::NewLine
        $tstr = $tstr + "Caption                                  :" +
$obj.Caption + [System.Environment]::NewLine
        $tstr = $tstr + "CodePage                                 :" +
$obj.CodePage + [System.Environment]::NewLine
        $tstr = $tstr + "Comment                                  :" +
$obj.Comment + [System.Environment]::NewLine
        $tstr = $tstr + "CountryCode                              :" +
$obj.CountryCode + [System.Environment]::NewLine
        $tstr = $tstr + "Description                              :" +
$obj.Description + [System.Environment]::NewLine
        $tstr = $tstr + "Flags                                    :" +
$obj.Flags + [System.Environment]::NewLine
        $tstr = $tstr + "FullName                                 :" +
$obj.FullName + [System.Environment]::NewLine
        $tstr = $tstr + "HomeDirectory                            :" +
$obj.HomeDirectory + [System.Environment]::NewLine
        $tstr = $tstr + "HomeDirectoryDrive                       :" +
$obj.HomeDirectoryDrive + [System.Environment]::NewLine
        $tstr = $tstr + "LastLogoff                               :" +
$obj.LastLogoff + [System.Environment]::NewLine
        $tstr = $tstr + "LastLogon                                :" +
$obj.LastLogon + [System.Environment]::NewLine
        $tstr = $tstr + "LogonHours                               :" +
$obj.LogonHours + [System.Environment]::NewLine
        $tstr = $tstr + "LogonServer                              :" +
$obj.LogonServer + [System.Environment]::NewLine
        $tstr = $tstr + "MaximumStorage                           :" +
$obj.MaximumStorage + [System.Environment]::NewLine
        $tstr = $tstr + "Name                                     :" +
$obj.Name + [System.Environment]::NewLine
        $tstr = $tstr + "NumberOfLogons                           :" +
$obj.NumberOfLogons + [System.Environment]::NewLine
        $tstr = $tstr + "Parameters                               :" +
$obj.Parameters + [System.Environment]::NewLine
        $tstr = $tstr + "PasswordAge                              :" +
$obj.PasswordAge + [System.Environment]::NewLine
        $tstr = $tstr + "PasswordExpires                          :" +
$obj.PasswordExpires + [System.Environment]::NewLine
```

```
         $tstr = $tstr + "PrimaryGroupId                :" +
$obj.PrimaryGroupId + [System.Environment]::NewLine
         $tstr = $tstr + "Privileges                    :" +
$obj.Privileges + [System.Environment]::NewLine
         $tstr = $tstr + "Profile                       :" +
$obj.Profile + [System.Environment]::NewLine
         $tstr = $tstr + "ScriptPath                    :" +
$obj.ScriptPath + [System.Environment]::NewLine
         $tstr = $tstr + "SettingID                     :" +
$obj.SettingID + [System.Environment]::NewLine
         $tstr = $tstr + "UnitsPerWeek                  :" +
$obj.UnitsPerWeek + [System.Environment]::NewLine
         $tstr = $tstr + "UserComment                   :" +
$obj.UserComment + [System.Environment]::NewLine
         $tstr = $tstr + "UserId                        :" +
$obj.UserId + [System.Environment]::NewLine
         $tstr = $tstr + "UserType                      :" +
$obj.UserType + [System.Environment]::NewLine
         $tstr = $tstr + "Workstations                  :" +
$obj.Workstations + [System.Environment]::NewLine
         write-host $tstr
      }
      else
      {
         foreach($obj in $objs)
         {
             $tstr = $tstr + "AccountExpires            :" +
$obj.AccountExpires + [System.Environment]::NewLine
             $tstr = $tstr + "AuthorizationFlags        :" +
$obj.AuthorizationFlags + [System.Environment]::NewLine
             $tstr = $tstr + "BadPasswordCount          :" +
$obj.BadPasswordCount + [System.Environment]::NewLine
             $tstr = $tstr + "Caption                   :" +
$obj.Caption + [System.Environment]::NewLine
             $tstr = $tstr + "CodePage                  :" +
$obj.CodePage + [System.Environment]::NewLine
             $tstr = $tstr + "Comment                   :" +
$obj.Comment + [System.Environment]::NewLine
             $tstr = $tstr + "CountryCode               :" +
$obj.CountryCode + [System.Environment]::NewLine
             $tstr = $tstr + "Description               :" +
$obj.Description + [System.Environment]::NewLine
             $tstr = $tstr + "Flags                     :" +
$obj.Flags + [System.Environment]::NewLine
```

```
        $tstr = $tstr + "FullName                        :" +
$obj.FullName + [System.Environment]::NewLine
        $tstr = $tstr + "HomeDirectory                   :" +
$obj.HomeDirectory + [System.Environment]::NewLine
        $tstr = $tstr + "HomeDirectoryDrive              :" +
$obj.HomeDirectoryDrive + [System.Environment]::NewLine
        $tstr = $tstr + "LastLogoff                      :" +
$obj.LastLogoff + [System.Environment]::NewLine
        $tstr = $tstr + "LastLogon                       :" +
$obj.LastLogon + [System.Environment]::NewLine
        $tstr = $tstr + "LogonHours                      :" +
$obj.LogonHours + [System.Environment]::NewLine
        $tstr = $tstr + "LogonServer                     :" +
$obj.LogonServer + [System.Environment]::NewLine
        $tstr = $tstr + "MaximumStorage                  :" +
$obj.MaximumStorage + [System.Environment]::NewLine
        $tstr = $tstr + "Name                            :" +
$obj.Name + [System.Environment]::NewLine
        $tstr = $tstr + "NumberOfLogons                  :" +
$obj.NumberOfLogons + [System.Environment]::NewLine
        $tstr = $tstr + "Parameters                      :" +
$obj.Parameters + [System.Environment]::NewLine
        $tstr = $tstr + "PasswordAge                     :" +
$obj.PasswordAge + [System.Environment]::NewLine
        $tstr = $tstr + "PasswordExpires                 :" +
$obj.PasswordExpires + [System.Environment]::NewLine
        $tstr = $tstr + "PrimaryGroupId                  :" +
$obj.PrimaryGroupId + [System.Environment]::NewLine
        $tstr = $tstr + "Privileges                      :" +
$obj.Privileges + [System.Environment]::NewLine
        $tstr = $tstr + "Profile                         :" +
$obj.Profile + [System.Environment]::NewLine
        $tstr = $tstr + "ScriptPath                      :" +
$obj.ScriptPath + [System.Environment]::NewLine
        $tstr = $tstr + "SettingID                       :" +
$obj.SettingID + [System.Environment]::NewLine
        $tstr = $tstr + "UnitsPerWeek                    :" +
$obj.UnitsPerWeek + [System.Environment]::NewLine
        $tstr = $tstr + "UserComment                     :" +
$obj.UserComment + [System.Environment]::NewLine
        $tstr = $tstr + "UserId                          :" +
$obj.UserId + [System.Environment]::NewLine
        $tstr = $tstr + "UserType                        :" +
$obj.UserType + [System.Environment]::NewLine
```

```
            $tstr = $tstr + "Workstations                    :" +
$obj.Workstations + [System.Environment]::NewLine
            $tstr = $tstr + [System.Environment]::NewLine
        }
        write-host $tstr
    }
```

The wrong kind of wrong
This is where automation wins the day

LOVE TO AUTOMATE. THIS IS THE PLACE WHERE IT ISN'T JUST HELPFUL, IT IS A REQUIREMENT. There simply isn't anyway you can do what is needed without it. But not because the experience with Get-CIMInstance works the way everything else in the world of WMI works the same way. Rather, because it is the only way you are going to get full benefit from using it.

```
Get-CimInstance [-ClassName] <String> [-ComputerName <String[]>] [-
Filter <String>] [-KeyOnly] [-Namespace <String>] [-OperationTimeoutSec
<UInt32>] [-Property <String[]>]
    [-QueryDialect <String>] [-Shallow] [<CommonParameters>]

    Get-CimInstance [-Filter <String>] [-KeyOnly] [-Namespace <String>]
[-OperationTimeoutSec <UInt32>] [-Property <String[]>] [-Shallow] -
CimSession <CimSession[]> -ResourceUri
    <Uri> [<CommonParameters>]

    Get-CimInstance [-InputObject] <CimInstance> [-OperationTimeoutSec
<UInt32>]    [-ResourceUri    <Uri>]    -CimSession    <CimSession[]>
[<CommonParameters>]

    Get-CimInstance    [-Namespace    <String>]    [-OperationTimeoutSec
<UInt32>] [-QueryDialect <String>] [-ResourceUri <Uri>] [-Shallow] -
CimSession <CimSession[]> -Query <String>
    [<CommonParameters>]
```

```
    Get-CimInstance [-ClassName] <String> [-Filter <String>] [-KeyOnly]
[-Namespace    <String>]    [-OperationTimeoutSec    <UInt32>]    [-Property
<String[]>] [-QueryDialect <String>]
    [-Shallow] -CimSession <CimSession[]> [<CommonParameters>]

    Get-CimInstance [-ComputerName <String[]>] [-Filter <String>] [-
KeyOnly]   [-Namespace   <String>]   [-OperationTimeoutSec   <UInt32>]   [-
Property <String[]>] [-Shallow] -ResourceUri
    <Uri> [<CommonParameters>]

    Get-CimInstance [-ComputerName <String[]>] [-Namespace <String>] [-
OperationTimeoutSec  <UInt32>]  [-QueryDialect  <String>]  [-ResourceUri
<Uri>] [-Shallow] -Query <String>
    [<CommonParameters>]

    Get-CimInstance    [-InputObject]    <CimInstance>    [-ComputerName
<String[]>]   [-OperationTimeoutSec   <UInt32>]   [-ResourceUri   <Uri>]
[<CommonParameters>]
```

Yes, I know, yuck! So, let's keep it simple, shall we?

$objs = Get-CIMInstance -namespace root\cimV2 -Class Win32_Something

Those somethings are:

Win32_1394Controller	Win32_OfflineFilesSuspendInfo
Win32_1394ControllerDevice	Win32_OfflineFilesUserConfiguration
Win32_Account	Win32_OnBoardDevice
Win32_AccountSID	Win32_OperatingSystem
Win32_ACE	Win32_OperatingSystemAutochkSetting
Win32_ActionCheck	Win32_OperatingSystemQFE
Win32_ActiveRoute	Win32_OptionalFeature
Win32_AllocatedResource	Win32_OSRecoveryConfiguration
Win32_ApplicationCommandLine	Win32_PageFile
Win32_ApplicationService	Win32_PageFileElementSetting
Win32_AssociatedProcessorMemory	Win32_PageFileSetting

Win32_AutochkSetting	Win32_PageFileUsage
Win32_BaseBoard	Win32_ParallelPort
Win32_BaseService	Win32_Patch
Win32_Battery	Win32_PatchFile
Win32_Binary	Win32_PatchPackage
Win32_BinSetageAction	Win32_PCMCIAController
Win32_BIOS	Win32_PhysicalMedia
Win32_BootConfiguration	Win32_PhysicalMemory
Win32_Bus	Win32_PhysicalMemoryArray
Win32_CacheMemory	Win32_PhysicalMemoryLocation
Win32_CDROMDrive	Win32_PingStatus
Win32_CheckCheck	Win32_PNPAllocatedResource
Win32_CIMLogicalDeviceCIMDataFile	Win32_PnPDevice
Win32_ClassicCOMApplicationClasses	Win32_PnPEntity
Win32_ClassicCOMClass	Win32_PnPSignedDriver
Win32_ClassicCOMClassSetting	Win32_PnPSignedDriverCIMDataFile
Win32_ClassicCOMClassSettings	Win32_PointingDevice
Win32_ClassInfoAction	Win32_PortableBattery
Win32_ClientApplicationSetting	Win32_PortConnector
Win32_ClusterShare	Win32_PortResource
Win32_CodecFile	Win32_POTSModem
Win32_CollectionStatistics	Win32_POTSModemToSerialPort
Win32_COMApplication	Win32_PowerManagementEvent
Win32_COMApplicationClasses	Win32_Printer
Win32_COMApplicationSettings	Win32_PrinterConfiguration
Win32_COMClass	Win32_PrinterController
Win32_ComClassAutoEmulator	Win32_PrinterDriver
Win32_ComClassEmulator	Win32_PrinterDriverDll
Win32_CommandLineAccess	Win32_PrinterSetting
Win32_ComponentCategory	Win32_PrinterShare
Win32_ComputerShutdownEvent	Win32_PrintJob
Win32_ComputerSystem	Win32_PrivilegesStatus

Win32_ComputerSystemEvent	Win32_Process
Win32_ComputerSystemProcessor	Win32_Processor
Win32_ComputerSystemProduct	Win32_ProcessStartTrace
Win32_COMSetting	Win32_ProcessStartup
Win32_Condition	Win32_ProcessStopTrace
Win32_ConnectionShare	Win32_ProcessTrace
Win32_ControllerHasHub	Win32_Product
Win32_CreateFolderAction	Win32_ProductCheck
Win32_CurrentProbe	Win32_ProductResource
Win32_CurrentTime	Win32_ProductSoftwareFeatures
Win32_DCOMApplication	Win32_ProgIDSpecification
Win32_DCOMApplicationAccessAllowedSetting	Win32_ProgramGroupContents
Win32_DCOMApplicationLaunchAllowedSetting	Win32_ProgramGroupOrItem
Win32_DCOMApplicationSetting	Win32_Property
Win32_DefragAnalysis	Win32_ProtocolBinding
Win32_DependentService	Win32_PublishComponentAction
Win32_Desktop	Win32_QuickFixEngineering
Win32_DesktopMonitor	Win32_QuotaSetting
Win32_DeviceBus	Win32_Refrigeration
Win32_DeviceChangeEvent	Win32_Registry
Win32_DeviceMemoryAddress	Win32_RegistryAction
Win32_DeviceSettings	Win32_Reliability
Win32_DfsNode	Win32_ReliabilityRecords
Win32_DfsNodeTarget	Win32_ReliabilityStabilityMetrics
Win32_DfsTarget	Win32_RemoveFileAction
Win32_Directory	Win32_RemoveIniAction
Win32_DirectorySpecification	Win32_ReserveCost
Win32_DiskDrive	Win32_RoamingProfileBackgroundUploadParams
Win32_DiskDrivePhysicalMedia	Win32_RoamingProfileMachineConfiguration
Win32_DiskDriveToDiskPartition	Win32_RoamingProfileSlowLinkParams

Win32_DiskPartition	Win32_RoamingProfileUserConfiguration
Win32_DiskQuota	Win32_RoamingUserHealthConfiguration
Win32_DisplayConfiguration	Win32_ScheduledJob
Win32_DisplayControllerConfiguration	Win32_SCSIController
Win32_DMAChannel	Win32_SCSIControllerDevice
Win32_DriverForDevice	Win32_SecurityDescriptor
Win32_DuplicateFileAction	Win32_SecurityDescriptorHelper
Win32_Environment	Win32_SecuritySetting
Win32_EnvironmentSpecification	Win32_SecuritySettingAccess
Win32_ExtensionInfoAction	Win32_SecuritySettingAuditing
Win32_Fan	Win32_SecuritySettingGroup
Win32_FileSpecification	Win32_SecuritySettingOfLogicalFile
Win32_FloppyController	Win32_SecuritySettingOfLogicalShare
Win32_FloppyDrive	Win32_SecuritySettingOfObject
Win32_FolderRedirection	Win32_SecuritySettingOwner
Win32_FolderRedirectionHealth	Win32_SelfRegModuleAction
Win32_FolderRedirectionHealthConfiguration	Win32_SerialPort
Win32_FolderRedirectionUserConfiguration	Win32_SerialPortConfiguration
Win32_FontInfoAction	Win32_SerialPortSetting
Win32_Group	Win32_ServerConnection
Win32_GroupInDomain	Win32_ServerFeature
Win32_GroupUser	Win32_ServerSession
Win32_HeatPipe	Win32_Service
Win32_IDEController	Win32_ServiceControl
Win32_IDEControllerDevice	Win32_ServiceSpecification
Win32_ImplementedCategory	Win32_ServiceSpecificationService
Win32_InfraredDevice	Win32_Session
Win32_IniFileSpecification	Win32_SessionConnection
Win32_InstalledProgramFramework	Win32_SessionProcess
Win32_InstalledSoftwareElement	Win32_SessionResource
Win32_InstalledStoreProgram	Win32_SettingCheck

Win32_InstalledWin32Program	Win32_ShadowBy
Win32_IP4PersistedRouteTable	Win32_ShadowContext
Win32_IP4RouteTable	Win32_ShadowCopy
Win32_IP4RouteTableEvent	Win32_ShadowDiffVolumeSupport
Win32_IRQResource	Win32_ShadowFor
Win32_JobObjectStatus	Win32_ShadowOn
Win32_Keyboard	Win32_ShadowProvider
Win32_LaunchCondition	Win32_ShadowStorage
Win32_LoadOrderGroup	Win32_ShadowVolumeSupport
Win32_LoadOrderGroupServiceDependencies	Win32_Share
Win32_LoadOrderGroupServiceMembers	Win32_ShareToDirectory
Win32_LocalTime	Win32_ShortcutAction
Win32_LoggedOnUser	Win32_ShortcutFile
Win32_LogicalDisk	Win32_ShortcutSAP
Win32_LogicalDiskRootDirectory	Win32_SID
Win32_LogicalDiskToPartition	Win32_SIDandAttributes
Win32_LogicalFileAccess	Win32_SMBIOSMemory
Win32_LogicalFileAuditing	Win32_SoftwareElement
Win32_LogicalFileGroup	Win32_SoftwareElementAction
Win32_LogicalFileOwner	Win32_SoftwareElementCheck
Win32_LogicalFileSecuritySetting	Win32_SoftwareElementCondition
Win32_LogicalProgramGroup	Win32_SoftwareElementResource
Win32_LogicalProgramGroupDirectory	Win32_SoftwareFeature
Win32_LogicalProgramGroupItem	Win32_SoftwareFeatureAction
Win32_LogicalProgramGroupItemDataFile	Win32_SoftwareFeatureCheck
Win32_LogicalShareAccess	Win32_SoftwareFeatureParent
Win32_LogicalShareAuditing	Win32_SoftwareFeatureSoftwareElements
Win32_LogicalShareSecuritySetting	Win32_SoundDevice
Win32_LogonSession	Win32_StartupCommand
Win32_LogonSessionMappedDisk	Win32_SubDirectory
Win32_LUID	Win32_SubSession

Win32_LUIDandAttributes	Win32_SystemAccount
Win32_ManagedSystemElementResource	Win32_SystemBIOS
Win32_MappedLogicalDisk	Win32_SystemBootConfiguration
Win32_MemoryArray	Win32_SystemConfigurationChangeEvent
Win32_MemoryArrayLocation	Win32_SystemDesktop
Win32_MemoryDevice	Win32_SystemDevices
Win32_MemoryDeviceArray	Win32_SystemDriver
Win32_MemoryDeviceLocation	Win32_SystemDriverPNPEntity
Win32_MethodParameterClass	Win32_SystemEnclosure
Win32_MIMEInfoAction	Win32_SystemLoadOrderGroups
Win32_ModuleLoadTrace	Win32_SystemMemoryResource
Win32_ModuleTrace	Win32_SystemNetworkConnections
Win32_MotherboardDevice	Win32_SystemOperatingSystem
Win32_MountPoint	Win32_SystemPartitions
Win32_MoveFileAction	Win32_SystemProcesses
Win32_MSIResource	Win32_SystemProgramGroups
Win32_NamedJobObject	Win32_SystemResources
Win32_NamedJobObjectActgInfo	Win32_SystemServices
Win32_NamedJobObjectLimit	Win32_SystemSetting
Win32_NamedJobObjectLimitSetting	Win32_SystemSlot
Win32_NamedJobObjectProcess	Win32_SystemSystemDriver
Win32_NamedJobObjectSecLimit	Win32_SystemTimeZone
Win32_NamedJobObjectSecLimitSetting	Win32_SystemTrace
Win32_NamedJobObjectStatistics	Win32_SystemUsers
Win32_NetworkAdapter	Win32_TapeDrive
Win32_NetworkAdapterConfiguration	Win32_TCPIPPrinterPort
Win32_NetworkAdapterSetting	Win32_TemperatureProbe
Win32_NetworkClient	Win32_TerminalService
Win32_NetworkConnection	Win32_Thread
Win32_NetworkLoginProfile	Win32_ThreadStartTrace
Win32_NetworkProtocol	Win32_ThreadStopTrace
Win32_NTDomain	Win32_ThreadTrace

Win32_NTEventlogFile	Win32_TimeZone
Win32_NTLogEvent	Win32_TokenGroups
Win32_NTLogEventComputer	Win32_TokenPrivileges
Win32_NTLogEventLog	Win32_Trustee
Win32_NTLogEventUser	Win32_TypeLibraryAction
Win32_ODBCAttribute	Win32_USBController
Win32_ODBCDataSourceAttribute	Win32_USBControllerDevice
Win32_ODBCDataSourceSpecification	Win32_USBHub
Win32_ODBCDriverAttribute	Win32_UserAccount
Win32_ODBCDriverSoftwareElement	Win32_UserDesktop
Win32_ODBCDriverSpecification	Win32_UserInDomain
Win32_ODBCSourceAttribute	Win32_UserProfile
Win32_ODBCTranslatorSpecification	Win32_UserStateConfigurationControls
Win32_OfflineFilesAssociatedItems	Win32_UTCTime
Win32_OfflineFilesBackgroundSync	Win32_VideoConfiguration
Win32_OfflineFilesCache	Win32_VideoController
Win32_OfflineFilesChangeInfo	Win32_VideoSettings
Win32_OfflineFilesConnectionInfo	Win32_VoltageProbe
Win32_OfflineFilesDirtyInfo	Win32_Volume
Win32_OfflineFilesDiskSpaceLimit	Win32_VolumeChangeEvent
Win32_OfflineFilesFileSysInfo	Win32_VolumeQuota
Win32_OfflineFilesHealth	Win32_VolumeQuotaSetting
Win32_OfflineFilesItem	Win32_VolumeUserQuota
Win32_OfflineFilesMachineConfiguration	Win32_WMIElementSetting
Win32_OfflineFilesPinInfo	Win32_WMISetting

Yes, there are a lot of these. However, these are also the most popular ones and these just happen to have some nice descriptions and details that might be worth looking at later when you have the time.

Right now, we're concerned with some programming issues.

- We know that the Get-CIMInstance works just like Get-WMIObject and so, we need to see if the $objs has a count to determine how to work with the Get-CIMInstance
- We also know that because of this, unless we want to write a ton more complex code, we're going to use the same logic that we did with the Get-WMIObject and use an array for names and one for values.
- But unlike Get-WMIObject, we must know in advance what the properties are and physically drive them into the code logic.

Since you don't know what is on your machine, what you can call It makes sense to start there.

Going Back to the Future

Building an inventory of Namespaces and classes that are on your computer

HAVE TO BE THE FIRST TO ADMIT THAT THE SCRIPTS BELOW WEREN'T WRITTEN IN POWERSHELL. So, here's how this works. Create a directory folder on the desktop first and then Copy and Paste them there before running the scripts. Run the Namespaces first, then the categories second and the classes last. Give each about a minute head start.

Namespaces.VBS

```
Dim fso
Dim l
Dim s


EnumNamespaces("root")


Sub EnumNamespaces(ByVal nspace)

Set ws = createobject("Wscript.Shell")
Set fso = CreateObject("Scripting.FilesystemObject")

If fso.folderExists(ws.currentDirectory & "\" & nspace) = false then
  fso.CreateFolder(ws.currentDirectory & "\" & nspace)
End If

On error Resume Next

   Set objs = GetObject("Winmgmts:\\.\" &  nspace).InstancesOf("___Namespace", &H20000)
```

```vbs
    If err.Number <> 0 Then
      err.Clear
      Exit Sub
    End If

    For each obj in objs

       EnumNamespaces(nspace & "\" & obj.Name)
    Next

    End Sub
```

Caregories.vbs

```vbs
Dim fso
Dim l
Dim s

Set ws = createobject("Wscript.Shell")
Set fso = CreateObject("Scripting.FilesystemObject")

EnumNamespaces("root")


Sub EnumNamespaces(ByVal nspace)

EnumCategories(nspace)

If fso.folderExists(ws.currentDirectory & "\" & nspace) = false then
 fso.CreateFolder(ws.currentDirectory & "\" & nspace)
End If

On error Resume Next

Set objs = GetObject("Winmgmts:\\.\" &    nspace).InstancesOf("__Namespace",
&H20000)

If err.Number <> 0 Then
 err.Clear
 Exit Sub
End If
```

```vbscript
For each obj in objs

    EnumNamespaces(nspace & "\" & obj.Name)

Next

End Sub

Sub EnumCategories(ByVal nspace)

Set ws = createobject("Wscript.Shell")
Set fso = CreateObject("Scripting.FilesystemObject")

Set objs = GetObject("Winmgmts:\\.\" & nspace).SubClassesOf("", &H20000)
For each obj in objs

    pos = instr(obj.Path_.class, "_")

    if pos = 0 then
        If fso.folderExists(ws.currentDirectory & "\" & nspace & "\" & obj.Path_.Class) =
false then
            fso.CreateFolder(ws.currentDirectory & "\" & nspace & "\" & obj.Path_.Class)
        End If
    else
        if pos = 1 then
            If fso.folderExists(ws.currentDirectory & "\" & nspace & "\SuperClasses") =
false then
                fso.CreateFolder(ws.currentDirectory & "\" & nspace & "\SuperClasses")
            End If
        else
            If    fso.folderExists(ws.currentDirectory    &    "\"    &    nspace    &    "\"    &
Mid(obj.Path_.Class, 1, pos-1)) = false then
                fso.CreateFolder(ws.currentDirectory    &    "\"    &    nspace    &    "\"    &
Mid(obj.Path_.Class, 1, pos-1))
            End If
        End If
    End If

Next
```

```
End Sub
```

Classes.vbs

```vbs
Dim fso
Dim l
Dim s

EnumNamespaces("root")

Sub EnumNamespaces(ByVal nspace)

EnumClasses(nspace)

Set ws = createobject("Wscript.Shell")
Set fso = CreateObject("Scripting.FilesystemObject")

If fso.folderExists(ws.currentDirectory & "\" & nspace) = false then
 fso.CreateFolder(ws.currentDirectory & "\" & nspace)
End If

On error Resume Next

Set objs = GetObject("Winmgmts:\\.\" &    nspace).InstancesOf("__Namespace",
&H20000)

If err.Number <> 0 Then
  err.Clear
  Exit Sub
End If

For each obj in objs

   EnumNamespaces(nspace & "\" & obj.Name)

Next

End Sub
```

```
Sub EnumClasses(ByVal nspace)

Set ws = createobject("Wscript.Shell")
Set fso = CreateObject("Scripting.FilesystemObject")

Set objs = GetObject("Winmgmts:\\.\" &  nspace).SubClassesOf("", &H20000)
For each obj in objs

   pos = instr(obj.Path_.class, "_")

   if pos = 0 then
      call CreateXMLFile(ws.CurrentDirectory & "\" & nspace & "\" & obj.Path_.Class,
nspace, obj.Path_.Class)
   else
     if pos = 1 then
        call  CreateXMlFile(ws.CurrentDirectory  &  "\"  &  nspace  &  "\Superclasses",
nspace, obj.Path_.Class)
      else
        call    CreateXMLFile(ws.CurrentDirectory   &   "\"   &   nspace   &   "\"   &
Mid(obj.Path_.Class, 1, pos-1), nspace, obj.Path_.Class)
      End If
   End If

Next

End Sub

Sub CreateXMLFile(ByVal Path, ByVal nspace, ByVal ClassName)



Set fso = CreateObject("Scripting.FileSystemObject")
Dim shorty
On error Resume Next
shorty = fso.GetFolder(Path).ShortPath
If err.Number <> 0 then
err.Clear
Exit Sub
End IF
```

```
set obj = GetObject("Winmgmts:\\.\" &  nspace).Get(classname)

Set txtstream = fso.OpenTextFile(Shorty & "\" & Classname & ".xml", 2, true, -2)
txtstream.WriteLine("<data>")
txtstream.WriteLine(" <NamespaceInformation>")
txtstream.WriteLine("   <namespace>" & nspace & "</namespace>")
txtstream.WriteLine("   <classname>" & classname & "</classname>")
txtstream.WriteLine(" </NamespaceInformation>")
txtstream.WriteLine(" <properties>")

for each prop in obj.Properties_
   txtstream.WriteLine("   <property Name = """ & prop.Name & """ IsArray=""" &
prop.IsArray & """ DataType = """ & prop.Qualifiers_("CIMType").Value & """/>")
Next
txtstream.WriteLine(" </properties>")
txtstream.WriteLine("</data>")
txtstream.close

End sub
```

Once you give them a while to run, like ten minutes total, you should see this:

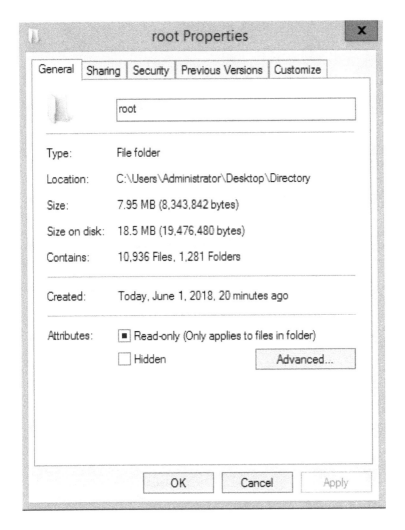

You could have more, or you could have less. Either way, you probably have never seen or thought there were that many classes before now.

May the power of WMI be with you!

Anyway, going to the root\CIMV2\Win32 folder, you will see the below files:

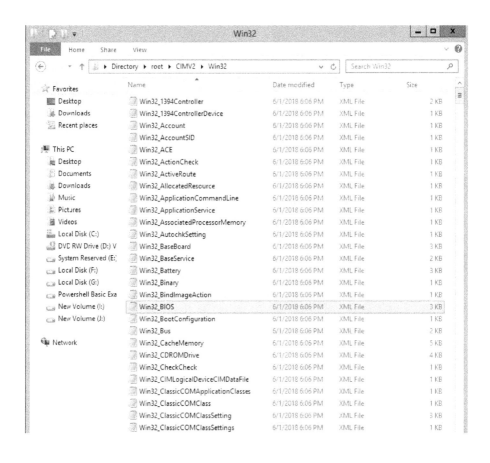

And the BIOS.xml looking like this:

```
Win32_BIOS - Notepad                                              _ □ X
File  Edit  Format  View  Help
<data>
  <NamespaceInformation>
    <namespace>root\CIMV2</namespace>
    <classname>Win32_BIOS</classname>
  </NamespaceInformation>
  <properties>
    <property Name = "BiosCharacteristics" IsArray="True" DataType = "uint16"/>
    <property Name = "BIOSVersion" IsArray="True" DataType = "string"/>
    <property Name = "BuildNumber" IsArray="False" DataType = "string"/>
    <property Name = "Caption" IsArray="False" DataType = "string"/>
    <property Name = "CodeSet" IsArray="False" DataType = "string"/>
    <property Name = "CurrentLanguage" IsArray="False" DataType = "string"/>
    <property Name = "Description" IsArray="False" DataType = "string"/>
    <property Name = "IdentificationCode" IsArray="False" DataType = "string"/>
    <property Name = "InstallableLanguages" IsArray="False" DataType = "uint16"/>
    <property Name = "InstallDate" IsArray="False" DataType = "datetime"/>
    <property Name = "LanguageEdition" IsArray="False" DataType = "string"/>
    <property Name = "ListOfLanguages" IsArray="True" DataType = "string"/>
    <property Name = "Manufacturer" IsArray="False" DataType = "string"/>
    <property Name = "Name" IsArray="False" DataType = "string"/>
    <property Name = "OtherTargetOS" IsArray="False" DataType = "string"/>
    <property Name = "PrimaryBIOS" IsArray="False" DataType = "boolean"/>
    <property Name = "ReleaseDate" IsArray="False" DataType = "datetime"/>
    <property Name = "SerialNumber" IsArray="False" DataType = "string"/>
    <property Name = "SMBIOSBIOSVersion" IsArray="False" DataType = "string"/>
    <property Name = "SMBIOSMajorVersion" IsArray="False" DataType = "uint16"/>
    <property Name = "SMBIOSMinorVersion" IsArray="False" DataType = "uint16"/>
    <property Name = "SMBIOSPresent" IsArray="False" DataType = "boolean"/>
    <property Name = "SoftwareElementID" IsArray="False" DataType = "string"/>
    <property Name = "SoftwareElementState" IsArray="False" DataType = "uint16"/>
    <property Name = "Status" IsArray="False" DataType = "string"/>
    <property Name = "TargetOperatingSystem" IsArray="False" DataType = "uint16"/>
    <property Name = "Version" IsArray="False" DataType = "string"/>
  </properties>
</data>
```

So, at this point we've profiled the classes and if we wanted to create programs from here without having to make WMI calls to pull up the need to know information to get the ball rolling.

Putting it all into motion

No time like now!

Okay, we are at that pivotal moment when we put all of this together so that we can accomplish something interesting. Let's work the arrays into the logic.

```
[Array]$Names
[Array]$Values


function WriteTheCode
{
  param
  (
  [Array]$Names,
  [Array]$Values,
  [string]$Classname
  )

  $tempstr = ""

  $ws = new-object -com WScript.Shell
  $fso = new-object -com Scripting.FileSystemObject
```

```
$txtstream = $fso.OpenTextFile($ws.CurrentDirectory + "\" + $Classname +
".csv", 2, $true, -2)

for($x=0;$x -lt $Names.GetLength(0); $x++)
{
    if($tempstr -ne "")
    {
      $tempstr = $tempstr + ","
    }
    $tempstr = $tempstr + $Names[$x]
}
$txtstream.WriteLine($tempstr)
$tempstr = ""
for($y=0;$y -lt $Values.GetLength(0); $y++)
{
    for($x=0;$x -lt $Names.GetLength(0); $x++)
    {
      if($tempstr -ne "")
      {
        $tempstr = $tempstr + ","
      }
      $tempstr = $tempstr + '"' + $Values[$y, $x] + '"'
    }
    $txtstream.WriteLine($tempstr)
    $tempstr = ""
}
$txtstream.Close()
$ws.run(($ws.CurrentDirectory + "\" + $Classname +  ".csv")

}

#This is where the program begins

$Namespace = "root\cimv2"
$Classname = "Win32_Process"
$l = new-object -com Wbemscripting.SWbemLocator
$svc = $l.ConnectServer(".", $Namespace)
$o = $svc.Get($Classname)

$objs = GET-CIMINSTANCE -namespace $Namespace -class $Classname
```

```powershell
if(!$objs.Count)
{
   $obj = $objs
   $Names=[Array]::CreateInstance([String], $o.Properties_.Count)
   $Values=[Array]::CreateInstance([String], 1, $o.Properties_.Count)

   $x = 0
   $y = 0

   foreach($prop in $o.Properties_)
   {
      $Names[$x] = $prop.Name
      $N = $prop.Name
      $p = $obj | Select -ExpandProperty $N
      $Values[0,$x] = $p
      $x = $x + 1
   }
}
else
{

   foreach($obj in $objs)
   {
      $Names=[Array]::CreateInstance([String], $o.Properties_.Count)
      $Values=[Array]::CreateInstance([String], $objs.Count, $o.Properties_.Count)
      break
   }
   $x = 0
   $y = 0


   foreach($obj in $objs)
   {

      foreach($prop in $o.Properties_)
      {
         $Names[$x] = $prop.Name
         $x = $x + 1
      }
      break
```

```
}
$x = 0
foreach($obj in $objs)
{
    foreach($prop in $o.Properties_)
    {
      $N = $prop.Name
      $p = $obj | Select -ExpandProperty $N
      $Values[$y, $x] = $p
      $x = $x + 1
    }
    $x=0
    $y = $y + 1
  }

}
WriteTheCode $Names $Values $Classname
```

And this produces:

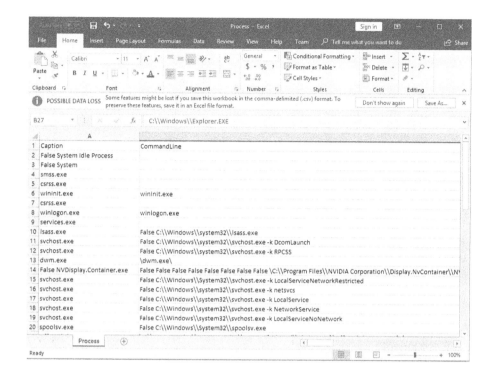

Of course, the code in the middle of the above routine can work on almost any kind of output.

Creating HTA Files

Reports and Tables

B

elow are HTA coding examples using the Get-CIMInstance cmdlet.

```
function WriteTheHTMLCode
{
        param
        (
        [Array]$Names,
        [Array]$Values,
        [String]$Tablename,
        [String]$TableType,
        [String]$Orientation,
        [String]$ControlType
        )

        $tempstr = ""

        $ws = new-object -com WScript.Shell
        $fso = new-object -com Scripting.FileSystemObject
        $txtstream = $fso.OpenTextFile($ws.CurrentDirectory + "\" + $Tablename
        + ".hta", 2, $true, -2)
        $txtstream.WriteLine("<html>")
```

```
$txtstream.WriteLine("<head>")
$txtstream.WriteLine("<HTA:APPLICATION ")
$txtstream.WriteLine("ID = ""Process"" ")
$txtstream.WriteLine("APPLICATIONNAME = """ & $Tablename  & """ ")
$txtstream.WriteLine("SCROLL = ""yes"" ")
$txtstream.WriteLine("SINGLEINSTANCE = ""yes"" ")
$txtstream.WriteLine("WINDOWSTATE = ""maximize"" >")
$txtstream.WriteLine("<title>" + $Tablename + "</title>")
$txtstream.WriteLine("<style type='text/css'>")
$txtstream.WriteLine("th")
$txtstream.WriteLine("{")
$txtstream.WriteLine("   COLOR: darkred;")
$txtstream.WriteLine("   BACKGROUND-COLOR: #eeeeee;")
$txtstream.WriteLine("   FONT-FAMILY:font-family: Cambria, serif;")
$txtstream.WriteLine("   FONT-SIZE: 12px;")
$txtstream.WriteLine("   text-align: left;")
$txtstream.WriteLine("   white-Space: nowrap;")
$txtstream.WriteLine("}")
$txtstream.WriteLine("td")
$txtstream.WriteLine("{")
$txtstream.WriteLine("   COLOR: navy;")
$txtstream.WriteLine("   BACKGROUND-COLOR: #eeeeee;")
$txtstream.WriteLine("   FONT-FAMILY: font-family: Cambria, serif;")
$txtstream.WriteLine("   FONT-SIZE: 12px;")
$txtstream.WriteLine("   text-align: left;")
$txtstream.WriteLine("   white-Space: nowrap;")
$txtstream.WriteLine("}")
$txtstream.WriteLine("div")
$txtstream.WriteLine("{")
$txtstream.WriteLine("   COLOR: white;")
$txtstream.WriteLine("   BACKGROUND-COLOR: navy;")
$txtstream.WriteLine("   FONT-FAMILY: font-family: Cambria, serif;")
$txtstream.WriteLine("   FONT-SIZE: 10px;")
$txtstream.WriteLine("   text-align: left;")
$txtstream.WriteLine("   white-Space: nowrap;")
$txtstream.WriteLine("}")
$txtstream.WriteLine("span")
$txtstream.WriteLine("{")
$txtstream.WriteLine("   COLOR: white;")
$txtstream.WriteLine("   BACKGROUND-COLOR: navy;")
```

```
$txtstream.WriteLine("   FONT-FAMILY: font-family: Cambria, serif;")
$txtstream.WriteLine("   FONT-SIZE: 10px;")
        $txtstream.WriteLine("   text-align: left;")
        $txtstream.WriteLine("   white-Space: nowrap;")
        $txtstream.WriteLine("   display:inline-block;")
        $txtstream.WriteLine("   width: 100%;")
        $txtstream.WriteLine("}")
        $txtstream.WriteLine("textarea")
        $txtstream.WriteLine("{")
        $txtstream.WriteLine("   COLOR: white;")
        $txtstream.WriteLine("   BACKGROUND-COLOR: navy;")
        $txtstream.WriteLine("   FONT-FAMILY: font-family: Cambria,
        serif;")
        $txtstream.WriteLine("   FONT-SIZE: 10px;")
        $txtstream.WriteLine("   text-align: left;")
        $txtstream.WriteLine("   white-Space: nowrap;")
        $txtstream.WriteLine("   width: 100%;")
        $txtstream.WriteLine("}")
        $txtstream.WriteLine("select")
        $txtstream.WriteLine("{")
        $txtstream.WriteLine("   COLOR: white;")
        $txtstream.WriteLine("   BACKGROUND-COLOR: navy;")
        $txtstream.WriteLine("   FONT-FAMILY: font-family: Cambria,
        serif;")
        $txtstream.WriteLine("   FONT-SIZE: 10px;")
        $txtstream.WriteLine("   text-align: left;")
        $txtstream.WriteLine("   white-Space: nowrap;")
        $txtstream.WriteLine("   width: 100%;")
        $txtstream.WriteLine("}")
        $txtstream.WriteLine("input")
        $txtstream.WriteLine("{")
        $txtstream.WriteLine("   COLOR: white;")
        $txtstream.WriteLine("   BACKGROUND-COLOR: navy;")
        $txtstream.WriteLine("   FONT-FAMILY: font-family: Cambria,
        serif;")
        $txtstream.WriteLine("   FONT-SIZE: 12px;")
        $txtstream.WriteLine("   text-align: left;")
        $txtstream.WriteLine("   display:table-cell;")
        $txtstream.WriteLine("   white-Space: nowrap;")
        $txtstream.WriteLine("}")
```

```
$txtstream.WriteLine("h1 {")
$txtstream.WriteLine("color: antiquewhite;")
$txtstream.WriteLine("text-shadow: 1px 1px 1px black;")
$txtstream.WriteLine("padding: 3px;")
$txtstream.WriteLine("text-align: center;")
$txtstream.WriteLine("box-shadow: invar 2px 2px 5px rgba(0,0,0,0.5),
invar -2px -2px 5px rgba(255,255,255,0.5);")
$txtstream.WriteLine("}")
$txtstream.WriteLine("</style>")

$txtstream.WriteLine("<body>")
$txtstream.WriteLine("</br>")

If($TableType -ne "Table")
{
    $txtstream.WriteLine("<table border='0' cellspacing='3'
cellpadding='3'>")
}
else
{
    $txtstream.WriteLine("<table border='1' cellspacing='3'
cellpadding='3'>")
}
if($Orientation -eq "Horizontal")
{

    $txtstream.WriteLine("<tr>")
    for($x=0;$x -lt $Names.GetLength(0); $x++)
    {
        $txtstream.WriteLine("<th align='Left' nowrap style='font-
family:Calibri, Sans-Serif;font-size: 12px;color:darkred'>" + $Names[$x] +
"</th>")
    }
    $txtstream.WriteLine("</tr>")

    for($y=0;$y -lt $Values.GetLength(0); $y++)
    {
        $txtstream.WriteLine("<tr>")
        for($x=0;$x -lt $Names.GetLength(0); $x++)
        {
```

```
            $tstr = $Values[$y,$x]
            switch($ControlType)
            {
                "None"{$txtstream.WriteLine("<td style='font-family:Calibri,
Sans-Serif;font-size:12px;color:navy;' align='left' nowrap='true'>" + $tstr
+ "</td>")break}
                "Div" {$txtstream.WriteLine("<td style='font-family:Calibri,
Sans-Serif;font-size:12px;color:navy;' align='left' nowrap='true'><div>" +
$tstr + "</div></td>")break}
                "Span"{$txtstream.WriteLine("<td style='font-family:Calibri,
Sans-Serif;font-size:12px;color:navy;' align='left' nowrap='true'><span>"
+ $tstr + "</span></td>")break}
                "Textarea"{$txtstream.WriteLine("<td style='font-
family:Calibri, Sans-Serif;font-size:12px;color:navy;' align='left'
nowrap='true'><textarea>" + $tstr + "</textarea></td>")break}
                "Textbox"{$txtstream.WriteLine("<td style='font-family:Calibri,
Sans-Serif;font-size:12px;color:navy;' align='left' nowrap='true'><input
type=text value="'" + $tstr + "'"></input></td>")break}

            }

        }
        $txtstream.WriteLine("</tr>")
    }

}
else
{
    for($x=0;$x -lt $Names.GetLength(0); $x++)
    {
        $txtstream.WriteLine("<tr><th align='Left' nowrap style='font-
family:Calibri, Sans-Serif;font-size: 12px;color:darkred'>" + $Names[$x] +
"</th>") break
        for($y=0;$y -lt $Values.GetLength(0); $y++)
        {
            $tstr = $Values[$y,$x]
            switch($ControlType)
            {
```

```
                "None"{$txtstream.WriteLine("<td style='font-family:Calibri,
Sans-Serif;font-size:12px;color:navy;' align='left' nowrap='true'>" + $tstr
+ "</td>")break}
                "Div" {$txtstream.WriteLine("<td style='font-family:Calibri,
Sans-Serif;font-size:12px;color:navy;' align='left' nowrap='true'><div>" +
$tstr + "</div></td>")break}
                "Span"{$txtstream.WriteLine("<td style='font-family:Calibri,
Sans-Serif;font-size:12px;color:navy;' align='left' nowrap='true'><span>"
+ $tstr + "</span></td>")break}
                "Textarea"{$txtstream.WriteLine("<td style='font-
family:Calibri, Sans-Serif;font-size:12px;color:navy;' align='left'
nowrap='true'><textarea>" + $tstr + "</textarea></td>")break}
                "Textbox"{$txtstream.WriteLine("<td align='left'
nowrap='true'><input style='font-family:Calibri, Sans-Serif;font-
size:12px;color:navy;' type=text value="""" + $tstr +
"""""></input></td>")break}
                }


            }
            $txtstream.WriteLine("</tr>")
        }
    }
    $txtstream.WriteLine("</table>")
    $txtstream.WriteLine("</body>")
    $txtstream.WriteLine("</html>")
    $txtstream.Close()

}
$Namespace = "root\cimv2"
$Classname = "Win32_Process"
$l = new-object -com Wbemscripting.SWbemLocator
$svc = $l.ConnectServer(".", $Namespace)
$o = $svc.Get($Classname)

$objs = GET-CIMINSTANCE -namespace $Namespace -class $Classname
if(!$objs.Count)
{
   $obj = $objs
   $Names=[Array]::CreateInstance([String], $o.Properties_.Count)
   $Values=[Array]::CreateInstance([String], 1, $o.Properties_.Count)
```

```
    $x = 0
    $y = 0

    foreach($prop in $o.Properties_)
    {
        $Names[$x] = $prop.Name
        $N = $prop.Name
        $p = $obj | Select -ExpandProperty $N
        $Values[0,$x] = $p
        $x = $x + 1
    }
}
else
{

    foreach($obj in $objs)
    {
        $Names=[Array]::CreateInstance([String], $o.Properties_.Count)
        $Values=[Array]::CreateInstance([String], $objs.Count, $o.Properties_.Count)
        break
    }
    $x = 0
    $y = 0


    foreach($obj in $objs)
    {

        foreach($prop in $o.Properties_)
        {
            $Names[$x] = $prop.Name
            $x = $x + 1
        }
        break
    }
    $x = 0
    foreach($obj in $objs)
    {
        foreach($prop in $o.Properties_)
```

```
    {
      $N = $prop.Name
      $p = $obj | Select -ExpandProperty $N
      $Values[$y, $x] = $p
      $x = $x + 1
    }
    $x=0
    $y = $y + 1
  }

}
WriteTheHTMLCode $Names $Values $Classname "Table" "Horizontal" "Textbox"
```

HTML with you in Mind
Reports and Tables and lots, lots more!

B

elow are HTML coding examples using the Get-CIMInstance cmdlet.

```
function WriteTheHTMLCode
{
    param
    (
    [Array]$Names,
    [Array]$Values,
    [String]$Tablename,
    [String]$TableType,
    [String]$Orientation,
    [String]$ControlType
    )

    $tempstr = ""

    $ws = new-object -com WScript.Shell
    $fso = new-object -com Scripting.FileSystemObject
    $txtstream = $fso.OpenTextFile($ws.CurrentDirectory + "\" + $Tablename +
".html", 2, $true, -2)
    $txtstream.WriteLine("<html>")
    $txtstream.WriteLine("<head>")
    $txtstream.WriteLine("<style type='text/css'>")
    $txtstream.WriteLine("th")
```

```
$txtstream.WriteLine("{")
$txtstream.WriteLine("    COLOR: darkred;")
$txtstream.WriteLine("    BACKGROUND-COLOR: #eeeeee;")
$txtstream.WriteLine("    FONT-FAMILY:font-family: Cambria, serif;")
$txtstream.WriteLine("    FONT-SIZE: 12px;")
$txtstream.WriteLine("    text-align: left;")
$txtstream.WriteLine("    white-Space: nowrap;")
$txtstream.WriteLine("}")
$txtstream.WriteLine("td")
$txtstream.WriteLine("{")
$txtstream.WriteLine("    COLOR: navy;")
$txtstream.WriteLine("    BACKGROUND-COLOR: #eeeeee;")
$txtstream.WriteLine("    FONT-FAMILY: font-family: Cambria, serif;")
$txtstream.WriteLine("    FONT-SIZE: 12px;")
$txtstream.WriteLine("    text-align: left;")
$txtstream.WriteLine("    white-Space: nowrap;")
$txtstream.WriteLine("}")
$txtstream.WriteLine("div")
$txtstream.WriteLine("{")
$txtstream.WriteLine("    COLOR: white;")
$txtstream.WriteLine("    BACKGROUND-COLOR: navy;")
$txtstream.WriteLine("    FONT-FAMILY: font-family: Cambria, serif;")
$txtstream.WriteLine("    FONT-SIZE: 10px;")
$txtstream.WriteLine("    text-align: left;")
$txtstream.WriteLine("    white-Space: nowrap;")
$txtstream.WriteLine("}")
$txtstream.WriteLine("span")
$txtstream.WriteLine("{")
$txtstream.WriteLine("    COLOR: white;")
$txtstream.WriteLine("    BACKGROUND-COLOR: navy;")
$txtstream.WriteLine("    FONT-FAMILY: font-family: Cambria, serif;")
$txtstream.WriteLine("    FONT-SIZE: 10px;")
$txtstream.WriteLine("    text-align: left;")
$txtstream.WriteLine("    white-Space: nowrap;")
$txtstream.WriteLine("    display:inline-block;")
$txtstream.WriteLine("    width: 100%;")
$txtstream.WriteLine("}")
$txtstream.WriteLine("textarea")
$txtstream.WriteLine("{")
$txtstream.WriteLine("    COLOR: white;")
```

```
$txtstream.WriteLine("   BACKGROUND-COLOR: navy;")
$txtstream.WriteLine("   FONT-FAMILY: font-family: Cambria, serif;")
$txtstream.WriteLine("   FONT-SIZE: 10px;")
$txtstream.WriteLine("   text-align: left;")
$txtstream.WriteLine("   white-Space: nowrap;")
$txtstream.WriteLine("   width: 100%;")
$txtstream.WriteLine("}")
$txtstream.WriteLine("select")
$txtstream.WriteLine("{")
$txtstream.WriteLine("   COLOR: white;")
$txtstream.WriteLine("   BACKGROUND-COLOR: navy;")
$txtstream.WriteLine("   FONT-FAMILY: font-family: Cambria, serif;")
$txtstream.WriteLine("   FONT-SIZE: 10px;")
$txtstream.WriteLine("   text-align: left;")
$txtstream.WriteLine("   white-Space: nowrap;")
$txtstream.WriteLine("   width: 100%;")
$txtstream.WriteLine("}")
$txtstream.WriteLine("input")
$txtstream.WriteLine("{")
$txtstream.WriteLine("   COLOR: white;")
$txtstream.WriteLine("   BACKGROUND-COLOR: navy;")
$txtstream.WriteLine("   FONT-FAMILY: font-family: Cambria, serif;")
$txtstream.WriteLine("   FONT-SIZE: 12px;")
$txtstream.WriteLine("   text-align: left;")
$txtstream.WriteLine("   display:table-cell;")
$txtstream.WriteLine("   white-Space: nowrap;")
$txtstream.WriteLine("}")
$txtstream.WriteLine("h1 {")
$txtstream.WriteLine("color: antiquewhite;")
$txtstream.WriteLine("text-shadow: 1px 1px 1px black;")
$txtstream.WriteLine("padding: 3px;")
$txtstream.WriteLine("text-align: center;")
$txtstream.WriteLine("box-shadow: invar 2px 2px 5px rgba(0,0,0,0.5), invar -2px
-2px 5px rgba(255,255,255,0.5);")
$txtstream.WriteLine("}")
$txtstream.WriteLine("</style>")
$txtstream.WriteLine("<title>" + $Tablename + "</title>")
$txtstream.WriteLine("</head>")
$txtstream.WriteLine("<body>")
$txtstream.WriteLine("</br>")
```

```
if($TableType -ne "Table")
{
    $txtstream.WriteLine("<table border='0' cellspacing='3' cellpadding='3'>")
}
else
{
    $txtstream.WriteLine("<table border='1' cellspacing='3' cellpadding='3'>")
}
if($Orientation -eq "Horizontal")
{
    $txtstream.WriteLine("<tr>")
    for($x=0;$x -lt $Names.GetLength(0); $x++)
    {
        $txtstream.WriteLine("<th align='Left' nowrap style='font-family:Calibri,
Sans-Serif;font-size: 12px;color:darkred'>" + $Names[$x] + "</th>")
    }
    $txtstream.WriteLine("</tr>")
    for($y=0;$y -lt $Values.GetLength(0); $y++)
    {
        $txtstream.WriteLine("<tr>")
        for($x=0;$x -lt $Names.GetLength(0); $x++)
        {
            $tstr = $Values[$y,$x]
            switch($ControlType)
            {
                "None"{$txtstream.WriteLine("<td style='font-family:Calibri, Sans-
Serif;font-size:12px;color:navy;' align='left' nowrap='true'>" + $tstr +
"</td>")break}
                "Div" {$txtstream.WriteLine("<td style='font-family:Calibri, Sans-
Serif;font-size:12px;color:navy;' align='left' nowrap='true'><div>" + $tstr +
"</div></td>")break}
                "Span"{$txtstream.WriteLine("<td style='font-family:Calibri, Sans-
Serif;font-size:12px;color:navy;' align='left' nowrap='true'><span>" + $tstr +
"</span></td>")break}
                "Textarea"{$txtstream.WriteLine("<td style='font-family:Calibri, Sans-
Serif;font-size:12px;color:navy;' align='left' nowrap='true'><textarea>" + $tstr +
"</textarea></td>")break}
                "Textbox"{$txtstream.WriteLine("<td style='font-family:Calibri, Sans-
Serif;font-size:12px;color:navy;' align='left' nowrap='true'><input type=text
value="""" + $tstr + """"></input></td>")break}
```

```
                }
            }
        $txtstream.WriteLine("</tr>")
        }

    }
    else
    {
        for($x=0;$x -lt $Names.GetLength(0); $x++)
        {
            $txtstream.WriteLine("<tr><th align='Left' nowrap style='font-
family:Calibri, Sans-Serif;font-size: 12px;color:darkred'>" + $Names[$x] + "</th>")
break
            for($y=0;$y -lt $Values.GetLength(0); $y++)
            {
                $tstr = $Values[$y,$x]
                switch($ControlType)
                {
                    "None"{$txtstream.WriteLine("<td style='font-family:Calibri, Sans-
Serif;font-size:12px;color:navy;' align='left' nowrap='true'>" + $tstr +
"</td>")break}
                    "Div" {$txtstream.WriteLine("<td style='font-family:Calibri, Sans-
Serif;font-size:12px;color:navy;' align='left' nowrap='true'><div>" + $tstr +
"</div></td>")break}
                    "Span"{$txtstream.WriteLine("<td style='font-family:Calibri, Sans-
Serif;font-size:12px;color:navy;' align='left' nowrap='true'><span>" + $tstr +
"</span></td>")break}
                    "Textarea"{$txtstream.WriteLine("<td style='font-family:Calibri, Sans-
Serif;font-size:12px;color:navy;' align='left' nowrap='true'><textarea>" + $tstr +
"</textarea></td>")break}
                    "Textbox"{$txtstream.WriteLine("<td align='left' nowrap='true'><input
style='font-family:Calibri, Sans-Serif;font-size:12px;color:navy;' type=text
value='''" + $tstr + "'''></input></td>")break}
                }
            }
        $txtstream.WriteLine("</tr>")
        }
    }
    $txtstream.WriteLine("</table>")
    $txtstream.WriteLine("</body>")
```

```
    $txtstream.WriteLine("</html>")
    $txtstream.Close()

}


$Namespace = "root\cimv2"
$Classname = "Win32_Process"
$l = new-object -com Wbemscripting.SWbemLocator
$svc = $l.ConnectServer(".", $Namespace)
$o = $svc.Get($Classname)
$objs = GET-CIMINSTANCE -namespace $Namespace -class $Classname
if(!$objs.Count)
{
    $obj = $objs
    $Names=[Array]::CreateInstance([String], $o.Properties_.Count)
    $Values=[Array]::CreateInstance([String], 1, $o.Properties_.Count)

    $x = 0
    $y = 0

    foreach($prop in $o.Properties_)
    {
        $Names[$x] = $prop.Name
        $N = $prop.Name
        $p = $obj | Select -ExpandProperty $N
        $Values[0,$x] = $p
        $x = $x + 1
    }
}
else
{
    foreach($obj in $objs)
    {
        $Names=[Array]::CreateInstance([String], $o.Properties_.Count)
        $Values=[Array]::CreateInstance([String], $objs.Count, $o.Properties_.Count)
        break
    }

    $x = 0
    $y = 0
```

```
foreach($obj in $objs)
{

    foreach($prop in $o.Properties_)
    {
        $Names[$x] = $prop.Name
        $x = $x + 1
    }
    break
}
$x = 0
foreach($obj in $objs)
{

    foreach($prop in $o.Properties_)
    {
        $N = $prop.Name
        $p = $obj | Select -ExpandProperty $N
        $Values[$y, $x] = $p
        $x = $x + 1
    }
    $x=0
    $y = $y + 1
}


}
WriteTheHTMLCode $Names $Values $Classname "Table" "Horizontal" "Textbox"
```

And this produces:

Caption	CommandLine	CreationClassName
False System Idle Proces		Win32_Process
False System		Win32_Process
smss.exe		Win32_Process
csrss.exe		Win32_Process
wininit.exe	wininit.exe	Win32_Process
csrss.exe		Win32_Process
winlogon.exe	winlogon.exe	Win32_Process
services.exe		Win32_Process
lsass.exe	False C:\\Windows\\syst	Win32_Process
svchost.exe	False C:\\Windows\\syst	Win32_Process
svchost.exe	False C:\\Windows\\syst	Win32_Process
dwm.exe	\dwm.exe\	Win32_Process

And the Vertical View:

Caption	System Idle Process	System
CommandLine		
CreationClassName	Win32_Process	Win32_Process
CreationDate		06/02/2018 01:09:33
CSCreationClassName	Win32_ComputerSystem	Win32_ComputerSystem
CSName	WIN-VNQ7KUKQ4NE	WIN-VNQ7KUKQ4NE
Description	System Idle Process	System
ExecutablePath		
ExecutionState		

Let's Do Some XML

From humble beginnings

W E CAN DO XML, AS WELL. Wait, did that just rhyme? I would like to show you a couple of examples doing it. Both examples have Database provider support and can also be used as ADO and OLEDB data sources.

Element XML

The idea here is to keep the code simple and supportive of what the providers can work with.

```
function WriteTheXMLCode
{
 param
 (
 [Array]$Names,
 [Array]$Values,
 [String]$Tablename
 )

 $tempstr = ""

 $ws = new-object -com WScript.Shell
 $fso = new-object -com Scripting.FileSystemObject
```

```
    $txtstream = $fso.OpenTextFile($ws.CurrentDirectory + "\" + $Tablename +
".xml", 2, $true, -2)
    $txtstream.WriteLine("<?xml version='1.0' encoding='iso-8859-1'?>")
    $txtstream.WriteLine("<data>")
    for($y=0;$y -lt $Values.GetLength(0); $y++)
    {
        $txtstream.WriteLine("<" + $Tablename + ">")
        for($x=0;$x -lt $Names.GetLength(0); $x++)
        {
            $tstr = $Values[$y,$x]
            $txtstream.WriteLine("<" + $Names[$x] + ">" + $tstr + "</" +
$Names[$x] + ">")
        }
        $txtstream.WriteLine("</" + $Tablename + ">")
    }
    $txtstream.WriteLine("</data>")
    $txtstream.Close()
    }
}


#This is where the program begins

$Namespace = "root\cimv2"
$Classname = "Win32_Process"
$l = new-object -com Wbemscripting.SWbemLocator
$svc = $l.ConnectServer(".", $Namespace)
$o = $svc.Get($Classname)

$objs = GET-CIMINSTANCE -namespace $Namespace -class $Classname
if(!$objs.Count)
{
    $obj = $objs
    $Names=[Array]::CreateInstance([String], $o.Properties_.Count)
    $Values=[Array]::CreateInstance([String], 1, $o.Properties_.Count)

    $x = 0
    $y = 0

    foreach($prop in $o.Properties_)
    {
```

```
         $Names[$x] = $prop.Name
         $N = $prop.Name
         $p = $obj | Select -ExpandProperty $N
         $Values[0,$x] = $p
         $x = $x + 1
    }
}
else
{

    foreach($obj in $objs)
    {
       $Names=[Array]::CreateInstance([String], $o.Properties_.Count)
       $Values=[Array]::CreateInstance([String], $objs.Count, $o.Properties_.Count)
       break
    }
    $x = 0
    $y = 0


    foreach($obj in $objs)
    {

       foreach($prop in $o.Properties_)
       {
          $Names[$x] = $prop.Name
          $x = $x + 1
       }
       break
    }
    $x = 0
    foreach($obj in $objs)
    {
       foreach($prop in $o.Properties_)
       {
          $N = $prop.Name
          $p = $obj | Select -ExpandProperty $N
          $Values[$y, $x] = $p
          $x = $x + 1
       }
```

```
      $x=0
      $y = $y + 1
   }
}
WriteTheXMLCode $Names $Values $Classname
```

Here's what that looks like:

```xml
- <data>
  - <Process>
      <Caption>System Idle Process</Caption>
      <CommandLine/>
      <CreationClassName>Win32_Process</CreationClassName>
      <CreationDate/>
      <CSCreationClassName>Win32_ComputerSystem</CSCreationClassName>
      <CSName>WIN-VNQ7KUKQ4NE</CSName>
      <Description>System Idle Process</Description>
      <ExecutablePath/>
      <ExecutionState/>
      <Handle>0</Handle>
      <HandleCount>0</HandleCount>
      <InstallDate/>
      <KernelModeTime>1577399062500</KernelModeTime>
      <MaximumWorkingSetSize/>
      <MinimumWorkingSetSize/>
      <Name>Win32_Process</Name>
      <OSCreationClassName>Win32_OperatingSystem</OSCreationClassName>
    - <OSName>
        Microsoft Windows Server 2012 R2 Standard Evaluation|C:\\Windows|\\Device\\Harddisk1\\Partition2
      </OSName>
      <OtherOperationCount>0</OtherOperationCount>
      <OtherTransferCount>0</OtherTransferCount>
      <PageFaults>1</PageFaults>
      <PageFileUsage>0</PageFileUsage>
      <ParentProcessId>0</ParentProcessId>
      <PeakPageFileUsage>0</PeakPageFileUsage>
      <PeakVirtualSize>65536</PeakVirtualSize>
      <PeakWorkingSetSize>24</PeakWorkingSetSize>
      <Priority>0</Priority>
      <PrivatePageCount>0</PrivatePageCount>
      <ProcessId>0</ProcessId>
      <QuotaNonPagedPoolUsage>0</QuotaNonPagedPoolUsage>
      <QuotaPagedPoolUsage>0</QuotaPagedPoolUsage>
      <QuotaPeakNonPagedPoolUsage>0</QuotaPeakNonPagedPoolUsage>
      <QuotaPeakPagedPoolUsage>0</QuotaPeakPagedPoolUsage>
      <ReadOperationCount>0</ReadOperationCount>
      <ReadTransferCount>0</ReadTransferCount>
      <SessionId>0</SessionId>
      <Status/>
      <TerminationDate/>
      <ThreadCount>8</ThreadCount>
      <UserModeTime>0</UserModeTime>
      <VirtualSize>65536</VirtualSize>
      <WindowsVersion>6.3.9600</WindowsVersion>
      <WorkingSetSize>24</WorkingSetSize>
      <WriteOperationCount>0</WriteOperationCount>
      <WriteTransferCount>0</WriteTransferCount>
  </Process>
  -
```

Element XML For XSL

```
function WriteTheXMLCode
{
 param
 (
[Array]$Names,
[Array]$Values,
[String]$Tablename
 )

 $tempstr = ""

 $ws = new-object -com WScript.Shell
 $fso = new-object -com Scripting.FileSystemObject
 $txtstream  =  $fso.OpenTextFile($ws.CurrentDirectory + "\" + $Tablename  +
".xml", 2, $true, -2)
 $txtstream.WriteLine("<?xml version='1.0' encoding='iso-8859-1'?>")
 $txtstream.WriteLine("<?xml-stylesheet  type='text/xsl'  href='" + $Tablename +
".xsl'?>")
 $txtstream.WriteLine("<data>")
 for($y=0;$y -lt $Values.GetLength(0); $y++)
 {
    $txtstream.WriteLine("<" + $Tablename + ">")
    for($x=0;$x -lt $Names.GetLength(0); $x++)
    {
      $tstr = $Values[$y,$x]
      $txtstream.WriteLine("<" + $Names[$x] + ">" + $tstr + "</" + $Names[$x] +
">")
    }
    $txtstream.WriteLine("</" + $Tablename + ">")
```

```
  }
  $txtstream.WriteLine("</data>")
  $txtstream.Close()

}
$Namespace = "root\cimv2"
$Classname = "Win32_Process"
$l = new-object -com Wbemscripting.SWbemLocator
$svc = $l.ConnectServer(".", $Namespace)
$o = $svc.Get($Classname)

$objs = GET-CIMINSTANCE -namespace $Namespace -class $Classname
if(!$objs.Count)
{
   $obj = $objs
   $Names=[Array]::CreateInstance([String], $o.Properties_.Count)
   $Values=[Array]::CreateInstance([String], 1, $o.Properties_.Count)

   $x = 0
   $y = 0

   foreach($prop in $o.Properties_)
   {
      $Names[$x] = $prop.Name
      $N = $prop.Name
      $p = $obj | Select -ExpandProperty $N
      $Values[0,$x] = $p
      $x = $x + 1
   }
}
else
{

   foreach($obj in $objs)
   {
      $Names=[Array]::CreateInstance([String], $o.Properties_.Count)
      $Values=[Array]::CreateInstance([String], $objs.Count, $o.Properties_.Count)
      break
   }
   $x = 0
```

```
    $y = 0


    foreach($obj in $objs)
    {

        foreach($prop in $o.Properties_)
        {
          $Names[$x] = $prop.Name
          $x = $x + 1
        }
        break
    }
    $x = 0
    foreach($obj in $objs)
    {
        foreach($prop in $o.Properties_)
        {
          $N = $prop.Name
          $p = $obj | Select -ExpandProperty $N
          $Values[$y, $x] = $p
          $x = $x + 1
        }
        $x=0
        $y = $y + 1
    }
}
WriteTheXMLCode $Names $Values $Classname
```

Schema.XML

```
function WriteTheXMLCode
{
 param
 (
 [Array]$Names,
 [Array]$Values,
```

```
  [String]$Tablename
  )

  $tempstr = ""

  $ws = new-object -com WScript.Shell
  $fso = new-object -com Scripting.FileSystemObject
  $txtstream = $fso.OpenTextFile($ws.CurrentDirectory + "\" + $Tablename +
".xml", 2, $true, -2)
  $txtstream.WriteLine("<?xml version='1.0' encoding='iso-8859-1'?>")
  $txtstream.WriteLine("<data>")
  for($y=0;$y -lt $Values.GetLength(0); $y++)
  {
     $txtstream.WriteLine("<" + $Tablename + ">")
     for($x=0;$x -lt $Names.GetLength(0); $x++)
     {
        $tstr = $Values[$y,$x]
        $txtstream.WriteLine("<" + $Names[$x] + ">" + $tstr + "</" + $Names[$x] +
">")
     }
     $txtstream.WriteLine("</" + $Tablename + ">")
  }
  $txtstream.WriteLine("</data>")
  $txtstream.Close()

  $cn = new-object -com ADODB.Connection
  $cn.ConnectionString = "Provider=MSDAOSP;Data Source=Msxml2.DSOControl"
  $cn.Open()

  $rs = new-object -com ADODB.Recordset
  $rs.ActiveConnection = $cn
  $rs.Open($ws.CurrentDirectory + "\" + $Tablename + ".xml")
  $rs.Save($ws.CurrentDirectory + "\" + $Tablename + "Schema.xml", 1)

}

$Namespace = "root\cimv2"
$Classname = "Win32_Process"
$l = new-object -com Wbemscripting.SWbemLocator
$svc = $l.ConnectServer(".", $Namespace)
```

```
$o = $svc.Get($Classname)

$objs = GET-CIMINSTANCE -namespace $Namespace -class $Classname
if(!$objs.Count)
{
    $obj = $objs
    $Names=[Array]::CreateInstance([String], $o.Properties_.Count)
    $Values=[Array]::CreateInstance([String], 1, $o.Properties_.Count)

    $x = 0
    $y = 0

    foreach($prop in $o.Properties_)
    {
        $Names[$x] = $prop.Name
        $N = $prop.Name
        $p = $obj | Select -ExpandProperty $N
        $Values[0,$x] = $p
        $x = $x + 1
    }
}
else
{

    foreach($obj in $objs)
    {
        $Names=[Array]::CreateInstance([String], $o.Properties_.Count)
        $Values=[Array]::CreateInstance([String], $objs.Count, $o.Properties_.Count)
        break
    }
    $x = 0
    $y = 0


    foreach($obj in $objs)
    {

        foreach($prop in $o.Properties_)
        {
            $Names[$x] = $prop.Name
```

```
        $x = $x + 1
    }
    break
}
$x = 0
foreach($obj in $objs)
{
    foreach($prop in $o.Properties_)
    {
        $N = $prop.Name
        $p = $obj | Select -ExpandProperty $N
        $Values[$y, $x] = $p
        $x = $x + 1
    }
    $x=0
    $y = $y + 1
}
}
WriteTheXMLCode $Names $Values "Process"
```

XSL
The logical choice

I T SEEMS LOGICAL, SINCE I JUST SHOWED YOU HOW TO CREATE ELEMENT XML FOR XSL, TO INCLUDE A ROUTINE THAT PRODUCES XSL. There are four ways to do the rendering and all work to get the job done.

Single Line Horizontal

```
function WriteTheXSLCode
{
  param
  (
  [Array]$Names,
  [Array]$Values,
  [String]$Tablename
  )

  $tempstr = ""

  $ws = new-object -com WScript.Shell
  $fso = new-object -com Scripting.FileSystemObject
  $txtstream = $fso.OpenTextFile($ws.CurrentDirectory + "\" + $Tablename + ".xsl", 2, $true, -2)
  $txtstream.WriteLine("<?xml version='1.0' encoding='iso-8859-1'?>")
```

```
$txtstream.WriteLine("<xsl:stylesheet version='1.0'
xmlns:xsl='http://www.w3.org/1999/XSL/Transform'>")
$txtstream.WriteLine("<xsl:template match=""/"">")
$txtstream.WriteLine("<html>")
$txtstream.WriteLine("<head>")
$txtstream.WriteLine("<title>Products</title>")
$txtstream.WriteLine("<style type='text/css'>")
$txtstream.WriteLine("th")
$txtstream.WriteLine("{")
$txtstream.WriteLine("    COLOR: black;")
$txtstream.WriteLine("    BACKGROUND-COLOR: white;")
$txtstream.WriteLine("    FONT-FAMILY:font-family: Cambria, serif;")
$txtstream.WriteLine("    FONT-SIZE: 12px;")
$txtstream.WriteLine("    text-align: left;")
$txtstream.WriteLine("    white-Space: nowrap;")
$txtstream.WriteLine("}")
$txtstream.WriteLine("td")
$txtstream.WriteLine("{")
$txtstream.WriteLine("    COLOR: black;")
$txtstream.WriteLine("    BACKGROUND-COLOR: white;")
$txtstream.WriteLine("    FONT-FAMILY: font-family: Cambria, serif;")
$txtstream.WriteLine("    FONT-SIZE: 12px;")
$txtstream.WriteLine("    text-align: left;")
$txtstream.WriteLine("    white-Space: nowrap;")
$txtstream.WriteLine("}")
$txtstream.WriteLine("div")
$txtstream.WriteLine("{")
$txtstream.WriteLine("    COLOR: black;")
$txtstream.WriteLine("    BACKGROUND-COLOR: white;")
$txtstream.WriteLine("    FONT-FAMILY: font-family: Cambria, serif;")
$txtstream.WriteLine("    FONT-SIZE: 10px;")
$txtstream.WriteLine("    text-align: left;")
$txtstream.WriteLine("    white-Space: nowrap;")
$txtstream.WriteLine("}")
$txtstream.WriteLine("span")
$txtstream.WriteLine("{")
$txtstream.WriteLine("    COLOR: black;")
$txtstream.WriteLine("    BACKGROUND-COLOR: white;")
$txtstream.WriteLine("    FONT-FAMILY: font-family: Cambria, serif;")
$txtstream.WriteLine("    FONT-SIZE: 10px;")
```

```
$txtstream.WriteLine("    text-align: left;")
$txtstream.WriteLine("    white-Space: nowrap;")
$txtstream.WriteLine("    display:inline-block;")
$txtstream.WriteLine("    width: 100%;")
$txtstream.WriteLine("}")
$txtstream.WriteLine("textarea")
$txtstream.WriteLine("{")
$txtstream.WriteLine("    COLOR: black;")
$txtstream.WriteLine("    BACKGROUND-COLOR: white;")
$txtstream.WriteLine("    FONT-FAMILY: font-family: Cambria, serif;")
$txtstream.WriteLine("    FONT-SIZE: 10px;")
$txtstream.WriteLine("    text-align: left;")
$txtstream.WriteLine("    white-Space: nowrap;")
$txtstream.WriteLine("    width: 100%;")
$txtstream.WriteLine("}")
$txtstream.WriteLine("select")
$txtstream.WriteLine("{")
$txtstream.WriteLine("    COLOR: black;")
$txtstream.WriteLine("    BACKGROUND-COLOR: white;")
$txtstream.WriteLine("    FONT-FAMILY: font-family: Cambria, serif;")
$txtstream.WriteLine("    FONT-SIZE: 10px;")
$txtstream.WriteLine("    text-align: left;")
$txtstream.WriteLine("    white-Space: nowrap;")
$txtstream.WriteLine("    width: 100%;")
$txtstream.WriteLine("}")
$txtstream.WriteLine("input")
$txtstream.WriteLine("{")
$txtstream.WriteLine("    COLOR: black;")
$txtstream.WriteLine("    BACKGROUND-COLOR: white;")
$txtstream.WriteLine("    FONT-FAMILY: font-family: Cambria, serif;")
$txtstream.WriteLine("    FONT-SIZE: 12px;")
$txtstream.WriteLine("    text-align: left;")
$txtstream.WriteLine("    display:table-cell;")
$txtstream.WriteLine("    white-Space: nowrap;")
$txtstream.WriteLine("}")
$txtstream.WriteLine("h1 {")
$txtstream.WriteLine("color: antiquewhite;")
$txtstream.WriteLine("text-shadow: 1px 1px 1px black;")
$txtstream.WriteLine("padding: 3px;")
$txtstream.WriteLine("text-align: center;")
```

```powershell
    $txtstream.WriteLine("box-shadow: invar 2px 2px 5px rgba(0,0,0,0.5), invar -2px -2px 5px rgba(255,255,255,0.5);")
    $txtstream.WriteLine("}")
    $txtstream.WriteLine("</style>")
    $txtstream.WriteLine("</head>")
    $txtstream.WriteLine("<body>")
    $txtstream.WriteLine("<table             border=""0""          Cellpadding=""2"" cellspacing=""2"">")
    $txtstream.WriteLine("<tr>")
    for($x=0;$x -lt $Names.GetLength(0); $x++)
    {
        $txtstream.WriteLine("<th>" + $Names[$x] + "</th>")
    }
    $txtstream.WriteLine("</tr>")
     $txtstream.WriteLine("<tr>")
    for($x=0;$x -lt $Names.GetLength(0); $x++)
    {
        $txtstream.WriteLine("<td        align='left'    nowrap='true'><xsl:value-of select="" data/" + $Tablename + "/" + $Names[$x] + """"/></td>")
    }
    $txtstream.WriteLine("</tr>")
    $txtstream.WriteLine("</table>")
    $txtstream.WriteLine("</body>")
    $txtstream.WriteLine("</html>")
    $txtstream.WriteLine("</xsl:template>")
    $txtstream.WriteLine("</xsl:stylesheet>")
    $txtstream.Close()

    }

$Namespace = "root\cimv2"
$Classname = "Win32_Process"
$l = new-object -com Wbemscripting.SWbemLocator
$svc = $l.ConnectServer(".", $Namespace)
$o = $svc.Get($Classname)

$objs = GET-CIMINSTANCE -namespace $Namespace -class $Classname
if(!$objs.Count)
{
   $obj = $objs
```

```
$Names=[Array]::CreateInstance([String], $o.Properties_.Count)
$Values=[Array]::CreateInstance([String], 1, $o.Properties_.Count)

$x = 0
$y = 0

foreach($prop in $o.Properties_)
{
    $Names[$x] = $prop.Name
    $N = $prop.Name
    $p = $obj | Select -ExpandProperty $N
    $Values[0,$x] = $p
    $x = $x + 1
}
}
else
{

    foreach($obj in $objs)
    {
        $Names=[Array]::CreateInstance([String], $o.Properties_.Count)
        $Values=[Array]::CreateInstance([String], $objs.Count, $o.Properties_.Count)
        break
    }
    $x = 0
    $y = 0


    foreach($obj in $objs)
    {

        foreach($prop in $o.Properties_)
        {
            $Names[$x] = $prop.Name
            $x = $x + 1
        }
        break
    }
    $x = 0
    foreach($obj in $objs)
```

```
    {
        foreach($prop in $o.Properties_)
        {
            $N = $prop.Name
            $p = $obj | Select -ExpandProperty $N
            $Values[$y, $x] = $p
            $x = $x + 1
        }
        $x=0
        $y = $y + 1
    }
}


WriteTheXSLCode $Names $Values "Process"
```

Multi-Line Horizontal

```
function WriteTheXSLCode
{
param
(
[Array]$Names,
[Array]$Values,
[String]$Tablename
)

$tempstr = ""

$ws = new-object -com WScript.Shell
$fso = new-object -com Scripting.FileSystemObject
$txtstream = $fso.OpenTextFile($ws.CurrentDirectory + "\" + $Tablename +
".xsl", 2, $true, -2)
$txtstream.WriteLine("<?xml version='1.0' encoding='iso-8859-1'?>")
$txtstream.WriteLine("<xsl:stylesheet                    version='1.0'
xmlns:xsl='http://www.w3.org/1999/XSL/Transform'>")
$txtstream.WriteLine("<xsl:template match=""""/""""">")
$txtstream.WriteLine("<html>")
```

```
$txtstream.WriteLine("<head>")
$txtstream.WriteLine("<title>Products</title>")
$txtstream.WriteLine("<style type='text/css'>")
$txtstream.WriteLine("th")
$txtstream.WriteLine("{")
$txtstream.WriteLine("    COLOR: black;")
$txtstream.WriteLine("    BACKGROUND-COLOR: white;")
$txtstream.WriteLine("    FONT-FAMILY:font-family: Cambria, serif;")
$txtstream.WriteLine("    FONT-SIZE: 12px;")
$txtstream.WriteLine("    text-align: left;")
$txtstream.WriteLine("    white-Space: nowrap;")
$txtstream.WriteLine("}")
$txtstream.WriteLine("td")
$txtstream.WriteLine("{")
$txtstream.WriteLine("    COLOR: black;")
$txtstream.WriteLine("    BACKGROUND-COLOR: white;")
$txtstream.WriteLine("    FONT-FAMILY: font-family: Cambria, serif;")
$txtstream.WriteLine("    FONT-SIZE: 12px;")
$txtstream.WriteLine("    text-align: left;")
$txtstream.WriteLine("    white-Space: nowrap;")
$txtstream.WriteLine("}")
$txtstream.WriteLine("div")
$txtstream.WriteLine("{")
$txtstream.WriteLine("    COLOR: black;")
$txtstream.WriteLine("    BACKGROUND-COLOR: white;")
$txtstream.WriteLine("    FONT-FAMILY: font-family: Cambria, serif;")
$txtstream.WriteLine("    FONT-SIZE: 10px;")
$txtstream.WriteLine("    text-align: left;")
$txtstream.WriteLine("    white-Space: nowrap;")
$txtstream.WriteLine("}")
$txtstream.WriteLine("span")
$txtstream.WriteLine("{")
$txtstream.WriteLine("    COLOR: black;")
$txtstream.WriteLine("    BACKGROUND COLOR: white;")
$txtstream.WriteLine("    FONT-FAMILY: font-family: Cambria, serif;")
$txtstream.WriteLine("    FONT-SIZE: 10px;")
$txtstream.WriteLine("    text-align: left;")
$txtstream.WriteLine("    white-Space: nowrap;")
$txtstream.WriteLine("    display:inline-block;")
$txtstream.WriteLine("    width: 100%;")
```

```
$txtstream.WriteLine("}")
$txtstream.WriteLine("textarea")
$txtstream.WriteLine("{")
$txtstream.WriteLine("    COLOR: black;")
$txtstream.WriteLine("    BACKGROUND-COLOR: white;")
$txtstream.WriteLine("    FONT-FAMILY: font-family: Cambria, serif;")
$txtstream.WriteLine("    FONT-SIZE: 10px;")
$txtstream.WriteLine("    text-align: left;")
$txtstream.WriteLine("    white-Space: nowrap;")
$txtstream.WriteLine("    width: 100%;")
$txtstream.WriteLine("}")
$txtstream.WriteLine("select")
$txtstream.WriteLine("{")
$txtstream.WriteLine("    COLOR: black;")
$txtstream.WriteLine("    BACKGROUND-COLOR: white;")
$txtstream.WriteLine("    FONT-FAMILY: font-family: Cambria, serif;")
$txtstream.WriteLine("    FONT-SIZE: 10px;")
$txtstream.WriteLine("    text-align: left;")
$txtstream.WriteLine("    white-Space: nowrap;")
$txtstream.WriteLine("    width: 100%;")
$txtstream.WriteLine("}")
$txtstream.WriteLine("input")
$txtstream.WriteLine("{")
$txtstream.WriteLine("    COLOR: black;")
$txtstream.WriteLine("    BACKGROUND-COLOR: white;")
$txtstream.WriteLine("    FONT-FAMILY: font-family: Cambria, serif;")
$txtstream.WriteLine("    FONT-SIZE: 12px;")
$txtstream.WriteLine("    text-align: left;")
$txtstream.WriteLine("    display:table-cell;")
$txtstream.WriteLine("    white-Space: nowrap;")
$txtstream.WriteLine("}")
$txtstream.WriteLine("h1 {")
$txtstream.WriteLine("color: antiquewhite;")
$txtstream.WriteLine("text-shadow: 1px 1px 1px black;")
$txtstream.WriteLine("padding: 3px;")
$txtstream.WriteLine("text-align: center;")
$txtstream.WriteLine("box-shadow: invar 2px 2px 5px rgba(0,0,0,0.5), invar -
2px -2px 5px rgba(255,255,255,0.5);")
$txtstream.WriteLine("}")
$txtstream.WriteLine("</style>")
```

```
    $txtstream.WriteLine("</head>")
    $txtstream.WriteLine("<body>")
    $txtstream.WriteLine("<table            border=""0""          Cellpadding=""2""
cellspacing=""2"">")
    $txtstream.WriteLine("<tr>")
    for($x=0;$x -lt $Names.GetLength(0); $x++)
    {
       $txtstream.WriteLine("<th>" + $Names[$x] + "</th>")
    }
    $txtstream.WriteLine("</tr>")
    $txtstream.WriteLine("<xsl:for-each select=""data/" + $Tablename + """">")
    $txtstream.WriteLine("<tr>")
    for($x=0;$x -lt $Names.GetLength(0); $x++)
    {
       $txtstream.WriteLine("<td          align='left'    nowrap='true'><xsl:value-of
select=""" + $Names[$x]  + """/></td>")
    }
    $txtstream.WriteLine("</tr>")
    $txtstream.WriteLine("</xsl:for-each>")
    $txtstream.WriteLine("</table>")
    $txtstream.WriteLine("</body>")
    $txtstream.WriteLine("</html>")
    $txtstream.WriteLine("</xsl:template>")
    $txtstream.WriteLine("</xsl:stylesheet>")
    $txtstream.Close()

    }


$Namespace = "root\cimv2"
$Classname = "Win32_Process"
$l = new-object -com Wbemscripting.SWbemLocator
$svc = $l.ConnectServer(".", $Namespace)
$o = $svc.Get($Classname)

$objs = GET-CIMINSTANCE -namespace $Namespace -class $Classname
if(!$objs.Count)
{
   $obj = $objs
   $Names=[Array]::CreateInstance([String], $o.Properties_.Count)
   $Values=[Array]::CreateInstance([String], 1, $o.Properties_.Count)
```

```
      $x = 0
      $y = 0

      foreach($prop in $o.Properties_)
      {
         $Names[$x] = $prop.Name
         $N = $prop.Name
         $p = $obj | Select -ExpandProperty $N
         $Values[0,$x] = $p
         $x = $x + 1
      }
}
else
{

      foreach($obj in $objs)
      {
         $Names=[Array]::CreateInstance([String], $o.Properties_.Count)
         $Values=[Array]::CreateInstance([String], $objs.Count, $o.Properties_.Count)
         break
      }
      $x = 0
      $y = 0


      foreach($obj in $objs)
      {

         foreach($prop in $o.Properties_)
         {
            $Names[$x] = $prop.Name
            $x = $x + 1
         }
         break
      }
      $x = 0
      foreach($obj in $objs)
      {
         foreach($prop in $o.Properties_)
```

```
    {
        $N = $prop.Name
        $p = $obj | Select -ExpandProperty $N
        $Values[$y, $x] = $p
        $x = $x + 1
    }
    $x=0
    $y = $y + 1
    }
}
WriteTheXSLCode $Names $Values "Process"
```

Single Line Vertical

```
function WriteTheXSLCode
{
param
(
[Array]$Names,
[Array]$Values,
[String]$Tablename
)

$tempstr = ""

$ws = new-object -com WScript.Shell
$fso = new-object -com Scripting.FileSystemObject
$txtstream = $fso.OpenTextFile($ws.CurrentDirectory + "\" + $Tablename +
".xsl", 2, $true, -2)
$txtstream.WriteLine("<?xml version='1.0' encoding='iso-8859-1'?>")
$txtstream.WriteLine("<xsl:stylesheet                          version='1.0'
xmlns:xsl='http://www.w3.org/1999/XSL/Transform'>")
$txtstream.WriteLine("<xsl:template match=""/"">")
$txtstream.WriteLine("<html>")
$txtstream.WriteLine("<head>")
$txtstream.WriteLine("<title>Products</title>")
$txtstream.WriteLine("<style type='text/css'>")
$txtstream.WriteLine("th")
```

```
$txtstream.WriteLine("{")
$txtstream.WriteLine("   COLOR: black;")
$txtstream.WriteLine("   BACKGROUND-COLOR: white;")
$txtstream.WriteLine("   FONT-FAMILY:font-family: Cambria, serif;")
$txtstream.WriteLine("   FONT-SIZE: 12px;")
$txtstream.WriteLine("   text-align: left;")
$txtstream.WriteLine("   white-Space: nowrap;")
$txtstream.WriteLine("}")
$txtstream.WriteLine("td")
$txtstream.WriteLine("{")
$txtstream.WriteLine("   COLOR: black;")
$txtstream.WriteLine("   BACKGROUND-COLOR: white;")
$txtstream.WriteLine("   FONT-FAMILY: font-family: Cambria, serif;")
$txtstream.WriteLine("   FONT-SIZE: 12px;")
$txtstream.WriteLine("   text-align: left;")
$txtstream.WriteLine("   white-Space: nowrap;")
$txtstream.WriteLine("}")
$txtstream.WriteLine("div")
$txtstream.WriteLine("{")
$txtstream.WriteLine("   COLOR: black;")
$txtstream.WriteLine("   BACKGROUND-COLOR: white;")
$txtstream.WriteLine("   FONT-FAMILY: font-family: Cambria, serif;")
$txtstream.WriteLine("   FONT-SIZE: 10px;")
$txtstream.WriteLine("   text-align: left;")
$txtstream.WriteLine("   white-Space: nowrap;")
$txtstream.WriteLine("}")
$txtstream.WriteLine("span")
$txtstream.WriteLine("{")
$txtstream.WriteLine("   COLOR: black;")
$txtstream.WriteLine("   BACKGROUND-COLOR: white;")
$txtstream.WriteLine("   FONT-FAMILY: font-family: Cambria, serif;")
$txtstream.WriteLine("   FONT-SIZE: 10px;")
$txtstream.WriteLine("   text-align: left;")
$txtstream.WriteLine("   white-Space: nowrap;")
$txtstream.WriteLine("   display:inline-block;")
$txtstream.WriteLine("   width: 100%;")
$txtstream.WriteLine("}")
$txtstream.WriteLine("textarea")
$txtstream.WriteLine("{")
$txtstream.WriteLine("   COLOR: black;")
```

```
$txtstream.WriteLine("   BACKGROUND-COLOR: white;")
$txtstream.WriteLine("   FONT-FAMILY: font-family: Cambria, serif;")
$txtstream.WriteLine("   FONT-SIZE: 10px;")
$txtstream.WriteLine("   text-align: left;")
$txtstream.WriteLine("   white-Space: nowrap;")
$txtstream.WriteLine("   width: 100%;")
$txtstream.WriteLine("}")
$txtstream.WriteLine("select")
$txtstream.WriteLine("{")
$txtstream.WriteLine("   COLOR: black;")
$txtstream.WriteLine("   BACKGROUND-COLOR: white;")
$txtstream.WriteLine("   FONT-FAMILY: font-family: Cambria, serif;")
$txtstream.WriteLine("   FONT-SIZE: 10px;")
$txtstream.WriteLine("   text-align: left;")
$txtstream.WriteLine("   white-Space: nowrap;")
$txtstream.WriteLine("   width: 100%;")
$txtstream.WriteLine("}")
$txtstream.WriteLine("input")
$txtstream.WriteLine("{")
$txtstream.WriteLine("   COLOR: black;")
$txtstream.WriteLine("   BACKGROUND-COLOR: white;")
$txtstream.WriteLine("   FONT-FAMILY: font-family: Cambria, serif;")
$txtstream.WriteLine("   FONT-SIZE: 12px;")
$txtstream.WriteLine("   text-align: left;")
$txtstream.WriteLine("   display:table-cell;")
$txtstream.WriteLine("   white-Space: nowrap;")
$txtstream.WriteLine("}")
$txtstream.WriteLine("h1 {")
$txtstream.WriteLine("color: antiquewhite;")
$txtstream.WriteLine("text-shadow: 1px 1px 1px black;")
$txtstream.WriteLine("padding: 3px;")
$txtstream.WriteLine("text-align: center;")
$txtstream.WriteLine("box-shadow: invar 2px 2px 5px rgba(0,0,0,0.5), invar -2px -2px 5px rgba(255,255,255,0.5);")
$txtstream.WriteLine("}")
$txtstream.WriteLine("</style>")
$txtstream.WriteLine("</head>")
$txtstream.WriteLine("<body>")
$txtstream.WriteLine("<table        border=""0""         Cellpadding=""2"" cellspacing=""2"">")
```

```
$txtstream.WriteLine("<tr>")
for($x=0;$x -lt $Names.GetLength(0); $x++)
{
    $txtstream.WriteLine("<tr><th>" + $Names[$x] + "</th>")
    $txtstream.WriteLine("<td        align='left'    nowrap='true'><xsl:value-of
select="" data/" + $Tablename + "/" + $Names[$x]  + """"/></td></tr>")
}
$txtstream.WriteLine("</table>")
$txtstream.WriteLine("</body>")
$txtstream.WriteLine("</html>")
$txtstream.WriteLine("</xsl:template>")
$txtstream.WriteLine("</xsl:stylesheet>")
$txtstream.Close()

}
$Namespace = "root\cimv2"
$Classname = "Win32_Process"
$l = new-object -com Wbemscripting.SWbemLocator
$svc = $l.ConnectServer(".", $Namespace)
$o = $svc.Get($Classname)

$objs = GET-CIMINSTANCE -namespace $Namespace -class $Classname
if(!$objs.Count)
{
    $obj = $objs
    $Names=[Array]::CreateInstance([String], $o.Properties_.Count)
    $Values=[Array]::CreateInstance([String], 1, $o.Properties_.Count)

    $x = 0
    $y = 0

    foreach($prop in $o.Properties_)
    {
        $Names[$x] = $prop.Name
        $N = $prop.Name
        $p = $obj | Select -ExpandProperty $N
        $Values[0,$x] = $p
        $x = $x + 1
    }
}
```

```
else
{

   foreach($obj in $objs)
   {
      $Names=[Array]::CreateInstance([String], $o.Properties_.Count)
      $Values=[Array]::CreateInstance([String], $objs.Count, $o.Properties_.Count)
      break
   }
   $x = 0
   $y = 0


   foreach($obj in $objs)
   {

      foreach($prop in $o.Properties_)
      {
         $Names[$x] = $prop.Name
         $x = $x + 1
      }
      break
   }
   $x = 0
   foreach($obj in $objs)
   {
      foreach($prop in $o.Properties_)
      {
         $N = $prop.Name
         $p = $obj | Select -ExpandProperty $N
         $Values[$y, $x] = $p
         $x = $x + 1
      }
      $x=0
      $y = $y + 1
   }
}
WriteTheXSLCode $Names $Values "Process"
```

Multi-Line Vertical

```
function WriteTheXSLCode
{
 param
 (
 [Array]$Names,
 [Array]$Values,
 [String]$Tablename
 )

 $tempstr = ""

 $ws = new-object -com WScript.Shell
 $fso = new-object -com Scripting.FileSystemObject
 $txtstream = $fso.OpenTextFile($ws.CurrentDirectory + "\" + $Tablename +
".xsl", 2, $true, -2)
 $txtstream.WriteLine("<?xml version='1.0' encoding='iso-8859-1'?>")
 $txtstream.WriteLine("<xsl:stylesheet                              version='1.0'
xmlns:xsl='http://www.w3.org/1999/XSL/Transform'>")
 $txtstream.WriteLine("<xsl:template match=""/"">")
 $txtstream.WriteLine("<html>")
 $txtstream.WriteLine("<head>")
 $txtstream.WriteLine("<title>Products</title>")
 $txtstream.WriteLine("<style type='text/css'>")
 $txtstream.WriteLine("th")
 $txtstream.WriteLine("{")
 $txtstream.WriteLine("   COLOR: black;")
 $txtstream.WriteLine("   BACKGROUND-COLOR: white;")
 $txtstream.WriteLine("   FONT-FAMILY:font-family: Cambria, serif;")
 $txtstream.WriteLine("   FONT-SIZE: 12px;")
 $txtstream.WriteLine("   text-align: left;")
 $txtstream.WriteLine("   white-Space: nowrap;")
 $txtstream.WriteLine("}")
 $txtstream.WriteLine("td")
 $txtstream.WriteLine("{")
 $txtstream.WriteLine("   COLOR: black;")
 $txtstream.WriteLine("   BACKGROUND-COLOR: white;")
 $txtstream.WriteLine("   FONT-FAMILY: font-family: Cambria, serif;")
```

```
$txtstream.WriteLine("    FONT-SIZE: 12px;")
$txtstream.WriteLine("    text-align: left;")
$txtstream.WriteLine("    white-Space: nowrap;")
$txtstream.WriteLine("}")
$txtstream.WriteLine("div")
$txtstream.WriteLine("{")
$txtstream.WriteLine("    COLOR: black;")
$txtstream.WriteLine("    BACKGROUND-COLOR: white;")
$txtstream.WriteLine("    FONT-FAMILY: font-family: Cambria, serif;")
$txtstream.WriteLine("    FONT-SIZE: 10px;")
$txtstream.WriteLine("    text-align: left;")
$txtstream.WriteLine("    white-Space: nowrap;")
$txtstream.WriteLine("}")
$txtstream.WriteLine("span")
$txtstream.WriteLine("{")
$txtstream.WriteLine("    COLOR: black;")
$txtstream.WriteLine("    BACKGROUND-COLOR: white;")
$txtstream.WriteLine("    FONT-FAMILY: font-family: Cambria, serif;")
$txtstream.WriteLine("    FONT-SIZE: 10px;")
$txtstream.WriteLine("    text-align: left;")
$txtstream.WriteLine("    white-Space: nowrap;")
$txtstream.WriteLine("    display:inline-block;")
$txtstream.WriteLine("    width: 100%;")
$txtstream.WriteLine("}")
$txtstream.WriteLine("textarea")
$txtstream.WriteLine("{")
$txtstream.WriteLine("    COLOR: black;")
$txtstream.WriteLine("    BACKGROUND-COLOR: white;")
$txtstream.WriteLine("    FONT-FAMILY: font-family: Cambria, serif;")
$txtstream.WriteLine("    FONT-SIZE: 10px;")
$txtstream.WriteLine("    text-align: left;")
$txtstream.WriteLine("    white-Space: nowrap;")
$txtstream.WriteLine("    width: 100%;")
$txtstream.WriteLine("}")
$txtstream.WriteLine("select")
$txtstream.WriteLine("{")
$txtstream.WriteLine("    COLOR: black;")
$txtstream.WriteLine("    BACKGROUND-COLOR: white;")
$txtstream.WriteLine("    FONT-FAMILY: font-family: Cambria, serif;")
$txtstream.WriteLine("    FONT-SIZE: 10px;")
```

```
$txtstream.WriteLine("    text-align: left;")
$txtstream.WriteLine("    white-Space: nowrap;")
$txtstream.WriteLine("    width: 100%;")
$txtstream.WriteLine("}")
$txtstream.WriteLine("input")
$txtstream.WriteLine("{")
$txtstream.WriteLine("    COLOR: black;")
$txtstream.WriteLine("    BACKGROUND-COLOR: white;")
$txtstream.WriteLine("    FONT-FAMILY: font-family: Cambria, serif;")
$txtstream.WriteLine("    FONT-SIZE: 12px;")
$txtstream.WriteLine("    text-align: left;")
$txtstream.WriteLine("    display:table-cell;")
$txtstream.WriteLine("    white-Space: nowrap;")
$txtstream.WriteLine("}")
$txtstream.WriteLine("h1 {")
$txtstream.WriteLine("color: antiquewhite;")
$txtstream.WriteLine("text-shadow: 1px 1px 1px black;")
$txtstream.WriteLine("padding: 3px;")
$txtstream.WriteLine("text-align: center;")
$txtstream.WriteLine("box-shadow: invar 2px 2px 5px rgba(0,0,0,0.5), invar -
2px -2px 5px rgba(255,255,255,0.5);")
$txtstream.WriteLine("}")
$txtstream.WriteLine("</style>")
$txtstream.WriteLine("</head>")
$txtstream.WriteLine("<body>")
$txtstream.WriteLine("<table          border=""0""          Cellpadding=""2""
cellspacing=""2"">")
for($x=0;$x -lt $Names.GetLength(0); $x++)
{
    $txtstream.WriteLine("<tr><th>"  +  $Names[$x]  +  "</th><xsl:for-each
select=""data/" + $Tablename + """><td align='left' nowrap='true'><xsl:value-of
select=""" + $Names[$x] + """/></td></xsl:for-each></tr>")
}
$txtstream.WriteLine("</table>")
$txtstream.WriteLine("</body>")
$txtstream.WriteLine("</html>")
$txtstream.WriteLine("</xsl:template>")
$txtstream.WriteLine("</xsl:stylesheet>")
$txtstream.Close()
```

```powershell
    }
$Namespace = "root\cimv2"
$Classname = "Win32_Process"
$l = new-object -com Wbemscripting.SWbemLocator
$svc = $l.ConnectServer(".", $Namespace)
$o = $svc.Get($Classname)

$objs = GET-CIMINSTANCE -namespace $Namespace -class $Classname
if(!$objs.Count)
{
    $obj = $objs
    $Names=[Array]::CreateInstance([String], $o.Properties_.Count)
    $Values=[Array]::CreateInstance([String], 1, $o.Properties_.Count)

    $x = 0
    $y = 0

    foreach($prop in $o.Properties_)
    {
        $Names[$x] = $prop.Name
        $N = $prop.Name
        $p = $obj | Select -ExpandProperty $N
        $Values[0,$x] = $p
        $x = $x + 1
    }
}
else
{

    foreach($obj in $objs)
    {
        $Names=[Array]::CreateInstance([String], $o.Properties_.Count)
        $Values=[Array]::CreateInstance([String], $objs.Count, $o.Properties_.Count)
        break
    }
    $x = 0
    $y = 0


    foreach($obj in $objs)
```

```
{
    foreach($prop in $o.Properties_)
    {
      $Names[$x] = $prop.Name
      $x = $x + 1
    }
    break
  }
  $x = 0
  foreach($obj in $objs)
  {
    foreach($prop in $o.Properties_)
    {
      $N = $prop.Name
      $p = $obj | Select -ExpandProperty $N
      $Values[$y, $x] = $p
      $x = $x + 1
    }
    $x=0
    $y = $y + 1
  }
}
WriteTheXSLCode $Names $Values "Process"
```

When the Element XML for XSL xml file is clicked, it created this:

Caption	CommandLine
System Idle Process	
System	
smss.exe	
csrss.exe	
wininit.exe	wininit.exe
csrss.exe	
services.exe	
lsass.exe	C:\\Windows\\system32\\lsass.exe
svchost.exe	C:\\Windows\\system32\\svchost.exe -k DcomLaunch
winlogon.exe	winlogon.exe
svchost.exe	C:\\Windows\\system32\\svchost.exe -k RPCSS
dwm.exe	\dwm.exe\
NVDisplay.Container.exe	\C:\\Program Files\\NVIDIA Corporation\\Display.NvContainer\\NVDisplay.Container.exe\ -s
svchost.exe	C:\\Windows\\System32\\svchost.exe -k LocalServiceNetworkRestricted
svchost.exe	C:\\Windows\\system32\\svchost.exe -k netsvcs
svchost.exe	C:\\Windows\\system32\\svchost.exe -k LocalService
svchost.exe	C:\\Windows\\system32\\svchost.exe -k NetworkService
svchost.exe	C:\\Windows\\System32\\svchost.exe -k LocalSystemNetworkRestricted
svchost.exe	C:\\Windows\\system32\\svchost.exe -k LocalServiceNoNetwork
spoolsv.exe	C:\\Windows\\System32\\spoolsv.exe
svchost.exe	C:\\Windows\\system32\\svchost.exe -k apphost

Visualizations
CSS rendering of HTML

T HE IMAGES BELOW ARE THE RESULT OF THE USE OF THE CSS STYLESHEETS THAT WERE COMBINED WITH THE HTML CODE I WROTE PREVIOUSLY and are examples of the difference between reports and tables.

Report:

Table:

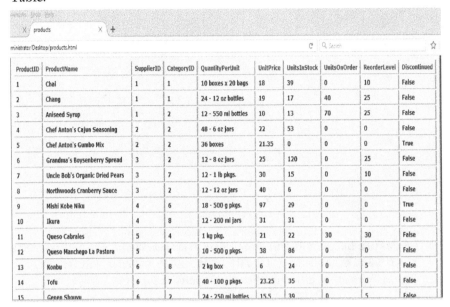

ProductID	ProductName	SupplierID	CategoryID	QuantityPerUnit	UnitPrice	UnitsInStock	UnitsOnOrder	ReorderLevel	Discontinued
1	Chai	1	1	10 boxes x 20 bags	18	39	0	10	False
2	Chang	1	1	24 - 12 oz bottles	19	17	40	25	False
3	Aniseed Syrup	1	2	12 - 550 ml bottles	10	13	70	25	False
4	Chef Anton's Cajun Seasoning	2	2	48 - 6 oz jars	22	53	0	0	False
5	Chef Anton's Gumbo Mix	2	2	36 boxes	21.35	0	0	0	True
6	Grandma's Boysenberry Spread	3	2	12 - 8 oz jars	25	120	0	25	False
7	Uncle Bob's Organic Dried Pears	3	7	12 - 1 lb pkgs.	30	15	0	10	False
8	Northwoods Cranberry Sauce	3	2	12 - 12 oz jars	40	6	0	0	False
9	Mishi Kobe Niku	4	6	18 - 500 g pkgs.	97	29	0	0	True
10	Ikura	4	8	12 - 200 ml jars	31	31	0	0	False
11	Queso Cabrales	5	4	1 kg pkg.	21	22	30	30	False
12	Queso Manchego La Pastora	5	4	10 - 500 g pkgs.	38	86	0	0	False
13	Konbu	6	8	2 kg box	6	24	0	5	False
14	Tofu	6	7	40 - 100 g pkgs.	23.25	35	0	0	False
15	Genen Shouyu	6	2	24 - 250 ml bottles	15.5	39	0	5	False

None:

Availability	BytesPerSector	Capabilities	CapabilityDescriptions	Caption	CompressionMethod	ConfigManagerErrorCode
	512	3, 4, 10	Random Access, Supports Writing, SMART Notification	OCZ REVODRIVE350 SCSI Disk Device		0
	512	3, 4	Random Access, Supports Writing	NVMe TOSHIBA-RD400		0
	512	3, 4, 10	Random Access, Supports Writing, SMART Notification	TOSHIBA Q701ACA200		0

Black and White

Availability	BytesPerSector	Capabilities	CapabilityDescriptions	Caption	CompressionMethod	ConfigManagerErrorCode	ConfigManagerUserConfig	CreationClassName	DefaultBlockSize	Description	DeviceID	ErrorCleared	ErrorDescription	ErrorMethodology
	512	3, 4, 10	Random Access, Supports	OC		0	FALSE	Win32_DiskDrive		Disk dri				
	512	3, 4	Random Access, Supports	NV		0	FALSE	Win32_DiskDrive		Disk dri				
	512	3, 4, 10	Random Access, Supports	NV		0	FALSE	Win32_DiskDrive		Disk dri				

Colored:

AccountExpires	AuthorizationFlags	BadPasswordCount	Caption	CodePage	Comment	CountryCode	Description
			NT AUTHORITY\SYSTEM				Network login profile settings for SYSTEM on NT AUTHORITY
			NT AUTHORITY\LOCAL SERVICE				Network login profile settings for LOCAL SERVICE on NT AUTHORITY
			NT AUTHORITY\NETWORK SERVICE				Network login profile settings for NETWORK SERVICE on NT AUTHORITY
	0	0	Administrator	0	Built-in account for administering the computer/domain	0	Network login profile settings for on WIN-UBLOAKMF3B
			NT SERVICE\SSASTELEMETRY				Network login profile settings for SSASTELEMETRY on NT SERVICE
			NT SERVICE\SSISTELEMETRY130				Network login profile settings for SSISTELEMETRY130 on NT SERVICE
			NT SERVICE\SQLTELEMETRY				Network login profile settings for SQLTELEMETRY on NT SERVICE
			NT SERVICE\MSSQLServerOLAPService				Network login profile settings for MSSQLServerOLAPService on NT SERVICE
			NT SERVICE\ReportServer				Network login profile settings for ReportServer on NT SERVICE
			NT SERVICE\MSSQLFDLauncher				Network login profile settings for MSSQLFDLauncher on NT SERVICE
			NT SERVICE\MSSQLLaunchpad				Network login profile settings for MSSQLLaunchpad on NT SERVICE
			NT SERVICE\SQLDtsServer130				Network login profile settings for SQLDtsServer130 on NT SERVICE
			NT SERVICE\MSSQLSERVER				Network login profile settings for MSSQLSERVER on NT SERVICE
			IIS APPPOOL\Classic .NET AppPool				Network login profile settings for Classic .NET AppPool on IIS APPPOOL
			IIS APPPOOL\.NET v4.5				Network login profile settings for .NET v4.5 on IIS APPPOOL
			IIS APPPOOL\.NET v2.0				Network login profile settings for .NET v2.0 on IIS APPPOOL
			IIS APPPOOL\.NET v4.5 Classic				Network login profile settings for .NET v4.5 Classic on IIS APPPOOL
			IIS APPPOOL\.NET v2.0 Classic				Network login profile settings for .NET v2.0 Classic on IIS APPPOOL

Oscillating

Availability	BytesPerSector	Capabilities	CapabilityDescriptions	Caption	CompressionMethod	ConfigManagerErrorCode	ConfigManagerUserConfig
	512	3, 4, 10	Random Access, Supports Writing, SMART Notification	OCZ REVODRIVE350 SCSI Disk Device		0	FALSE
	512	3, 4	Random Access, Supports Writing	NVMe TOSHIBA-RD400		0	FALSE
	512	3, 4, 10	Random Access, Supports Writing, SMART Notification	TOSHIBA DT01ACA200		0	FALSE

3D

Availability	BytesPerSector	Capabilities	CapabilityDescriptions	Caption	CompressionMethod	ConfigManagerErrorCode	ConfigManagerUserConfig	CreationClassName
	512	3, 4, 10	Random Access, Supports Writing, SMART Notification	OCZ REVODRIVE350 SCSI Disk Device		0	FALSE	Win32_DiskDrive
	512	3, 4	Random Access, Supports Writing	NVMe TOSHIBA-RD400		0	FALSE	Win32_DiskDrive
	512	3, 4, 10	Random Access, Supports Writing, SMART Notification	TOSHIBA DT01ACA200		0	FALSE	Win32_DiskDrive

Shadow Box:

Availability	BytesPerSector	Capabilities	CapabilityDescriptions	Caption	CompressionMethod	ConfigManagerErrorCode	ConfigManagerUserConfig	CreationClassName	DefaultBlockSize
	512	3, 4, 10	Random Access, Supports Writing, SMART Notification	OCZ REVODRIVE350 SCSI Disk Device		0	FALSE	Win32_DiskDrive	
	512	3, 4	Random Access, Supports Writing	NVMe TOSHIBA-RD400		0	FALSE	Win32_DiskDrive	
	512	3, 4, 10	Random Access, Supports Writing, SMART Notification	TOSHIBA DT01ACA200		0	FALSE	Win32_DiskDrive	

Shadow Box Single Line Vertical

BiosCharacteristics	7, 10, 11, 12, 15, 16, 17, 19, 23, 24, 25, 26, 27, 28, 29, 32, 33, 40, 42, 43, 48, 50, 58, 59, 64, 65, 66, 67, 68, 69, 70, 71, 72, 73, 74, 75, 76, 77, 78, 79
BIOSVersion	ALASKA - 1072009, 0504, American Megatrends - 5000C
BuildNumber	
Caption	0504
CodeSet	
CurrentLanguage	en|US|iso8859-1
Description	0504
IdentificationCode	
InstallableLanguages	3
InstallDate	
LanguageEdition	
ListOfLanguages	en|US|iso8859-1, fr|FR|iso8859-1, zh|CN|unicode, , , , ,
Manufacturer	American Megatrends Inc.
Name	0504
OtherTargetOS	
PrimaryBIOS	TRUE

Shadow Box Multi line Vertical

Property	Column 1	Column 2	Column 3
Availability			
BytesPerSector	512	512	512
Capabilities	3, 4, 10	3, 4	3, 4, 10
CapabilityDescriptions	Random Access, Supports Writing, SMART Notification	Random Access, Supports Writing	Random Access, Supports Writing, SMART Notification
Caption	OCZ REVODRIVE350 SCSI Disk Device	NVMe TOSHIBA-RD400	TOSHIBA DT01ACA200
CompressionMethod			
ConfigManagerErrorCode	0	0	0
ConfigManagerUserConfig	FALSE	FALSE	FALSE
CreationClassName	Win32_DiskDrive	Win32_DiskDrive	Win32_DiskDrive
DefaultBlockSize			
Description	Disk drive	Disk drive	Disk drive
DeviceID	\\.\PHYSICALDRIVE2	\\.\PHYSICALDRIVE1	\\.\PHYSICALDRIVE0
ErrorCleared			
ErrorDescription			
ErrorMethodology			
FirmwareRevision	2.90	57CZ4102	MX6OABB0
Index	2	1	0

Appendix A
Stylesheets

don't even pretend to be a stylesheet guru. These are here because I like the way they look and what they do behind the scenes to get the job done.

NONE

```
txtstream.WriteLine("<style type='text/css'>")
txtstream.WriteLine("th")
txtstream.WriteLine("{")
txtstream.WriteLine("    COLOR: white;")
txtstream.WriteLine("}")
txtstream.WriteLine("td")
txtstream.WriteLine("{")
txtstream.WriteLine("    COLOR: white;")
txtstream.WriteLine("}")
txtstream.WriteLine("</style>")
```

BLACK AND WHITE TEXT

```
$txtstream.WriteLine("<style type='text/css'>")
$txtstream.WriteLine("th")
$txtstream.WriteLine("{")
$txtstream.WriteLine("    COLOR: white;")
$txtstream.WriteLine("    BACKGROUND-COLOR: black;")
```

```
$txtstream.WriteLine("    FONT-FAMILY:font-family: Cambria, serif;")
$txtstream.WriteLine("    FONT-SIZE: 12px;")
$txtstream.WriteLine("    text-align: left;")
$txtstream.WriteLine("    white-Space: nowrap;")
$txtstream.WriteLine("}")
$txtstream.WriteLine("td")
$txtstream.WriteLine("{")
$txtstream.WriteLine("    COLOR: white;")
$txtstream.WriteLine("    BACKGROUND-COLOR: black;")
$txtstream.WriteLine("    FONT-FAMILY: font-family: Cambria, serif;")
$txtstream.WriteLine("    FONT-SIZE: 12px;")
$txtstream.WriteLine("    text-align: left;")
$txtstream.WriteLine("    white-Space: nowrap;")
$txtstream.WriteLine("}")
$txtstream.WriteLine("div")
$txtstream.WriteLine("{")
$txtstream.WriteLine("    COLOR: white;")
$txtstream.WriteLine("    BACKGROUND-COLOR: black;")
$txtstream.WriteLine("    FONT-FAMILY: font-family: Cambria, serif;")
$txtstream.WriteLine("    FONT-SIZE: 10px;")
$txtstream.WriteLine("    text-align: left;")
$txtstream.WriteLine("    white-Space: nowrap;")
$txtstream.WriteLine("}")
$txtstream.WriteLine("span")
$txtstream.WriteLine("{")
$txtstream.WriteLine("    COLOR: white;")
$txtstream.WriteLine("    BACKGROUND-COLOR: black;")
$txtstream.WriteLine("    FONT-FAMILY: font-family: Cambria, serif;")
$txtstream.WriteLine("    FONT-SIZE: 10px;")
$txtstream.WriteLine("    text-align: left;")
$txtstream.WriteLine("    white-Space: nowrap;")
$txtstream.WriteLine("    display:inline-block;")
$txtstream.WriteLine("    width: 100%;")
$txtstream.WriteLine("}")
$txtstream.WriteLine("textarea")
$txtstream.WriteLine("{")
$txtstream.WriteLine("    COLOR: white;")
$txtstream.WriteLine("    BACKGROUND-COLOR: black;")
$txtstream.WriteLine("    FONT-FAMILY: font-family: Cambria, serif;")
$txtstream.WriteLine("    FONT-SIZE: 10px;")
```

```
$txtstream.WriteLine("    text-align: left;")
$txtstream.WriteLine("    white-Space: nowrap;")
$txtstream.WriteLine("    width: 100%;")
$txtstream.WriteLine("}")
$txtstream.WriteLine("select")
$txtstream.WriteLine("{")
$txtstream.WriteLine("    COLOR: white;")
$txtstream.WriteLine("    BACKGROUND-COLOR: black;")
$txtstream.WriteLine("    FONT-FAMILY: font-family: Cambria, serif;")
$txtstream.WriteLine("    FONT-SIZE: 10px;")
$txtstream.WriteLine("    text-align: left;")
$txtstream.WriteLine("    white-Space: nowrap;")
$txtstream.WriteLine("    width: 100%;")
$txtstream.WriteLine("}")
$txtstream.WriteLine("input")
$txtstream.WriteLine("{")
$txtstream.WriteLine("    COLOR: white;")
$txtstream.WriteLine("    BACKGROUND-COLOR: black;")
$txtstream.WriteLine("    FONT-FAMILY: font-family: Cambria, serif;")
$txtstream.WriteLine("    FONT-SIZE: 12px;")
$txtstream.WriteLine("    text-align: left;")
$txtstream.WriteLine("    display:table-cell;")
$txtstream.WriteLine("    white-Space: nowrap;")
$txtstream.WriteLine("}")
$txtstream.WriteLine("h1 {")
$txtstream.WriteLine("color: antiquewhite;")
$txtstream.WriteLine("text-shadow: 1px 1px 1px black;")
$txtstream.WriteLine("padding: 3px;")
$txtstream.WriteLine("text-align: center;")
$txtstream.WriteLine("box-shadow: invar 2px 2px 5px rgba(0,0,0,0.5), invar -2px -2px 5px rgba(255,255,255,0.5);")
$txtstream.WriteLine("}")
$txtstream.WriteLine("</style>")
```

COLORED TEXT

```
$txtstream.WriteLine("<style type='text/css'>")
$txtstream.WriteLine("th")
$txtstream.WriteLine("{")
$txtstream.WriteLine("    COLOR: darkred;")
```

```
$txtstream.WriteLine("   BACKGROUND-COLOR: #eeeeee;")
$txtstream.WriteLine("   FONT-FAMILY:font-family: Cambria, serif;")
$txtstream.WriteLine("   FONT-SIZE: 12px;")
$txtstream.WriteLine("   text-align: left;")
$txtstream.WriteLine("   white-Space: nowrap;")
$txtstream.WriteLine("}")
$txtstream.WriteLine("td")
$txtstream.WriteLine("{")
$txtstream.WriteLine("   COLOR: navy;")
$txtstream.WriteLine("   BACKGROUND-COLOR: #eeeeee;")
$txtstream.WriteLine("   FONT-FAMILY: font-family: Cambria, serif;")
$txtstream.WriteLine("   FONT-SIZE: 12px;")
$txtstream.WriteLine("   text-align: left;")
$txtstream.WriteLine("   white-Space: nowrap;")
$txtstream.WriteLine("}")
$txtstream.WriteLine("div")
$txtstream.WriteLine("{")
$txtstream.WriteLine("   COLOR: white;")
$txtstream.WriteLine("   BACKGROUND-COLOR: navy;")
$txtstream.WriteLine("   FONT-FAMILY: font-family: Cambria, serif;")
$txtstream.WriteLine("   FONT-SIZE: 10px;")
$txtstream.WriteLine("   text-align: left;")
$txtstream.WriteLine("   white-Space: nowrap;")
$txtstream.WriteLine("}")
$txtstream.WriteLine("span")
$txtstream.WriteLine("{")
$txtstream.WriteLine("   COLOR: white;")
$txtstream.WriteLine("   BACKGROUND-COLOR: navy;")
$txtstream.WriteLine("   FONT-FAMILY: font-family: Cambria, serif;")
$txtstream.WriteLine("   FONT-SIZE: 10px;")
$txtstream.WriteLine("   text-align: left;")
$txtstream.WriteLine("   white-Space: nowrap;")
$txtstream.WriteLine("   display:inline-block;")
$txtstream.WriteLine("   width: 100%;")
$txtstream.WriteLine("}")
$txtstream.WriteLine("textarea")
$txtstream.WriteLine("{")
$txtstream.WriteLine("   COLOR: white;")
$txtstream.WriteLine("   BACKGROUND-COLOR: navy;")
$txtstream.WriteLine("   FONT-FAMILY: font-family: Cambria, serif;")
```

```
$txtstream.WriteLine("    FONT-SIZE: 10px;")
$txtstream.WriteLine("    text-align: left;")
$txtstream.WriteLine("    white-Space: nowrap;")
$txtstream.WriteLine("    width: 100%;")
$txtstream.WriteLine("}")
$txtstream.WriteLine("select")
$txtstream.WriteLine("{")
$txtstream.WriteLine("    COLOR: white;")
$txtstream.WriteLine("    BACKGROUND-COLOR: navy;")
$txtstream.WriteLine("    FONT-FAMILY: font-family: Cambria, serif;")
$txtstream.WriteLine("    FONT-SIZE: 10px;")
$txtstream.WriteLine("    text-align: left;")
$txtstream.WriteLine("    white-Space: nowrap;")
$txtstream.WriteLine("    width: 100%;")
$txtstream.WriteLine("}")
$txtstream.WriteLine("input")
$txtstream.WriteLine("{")
$txtstream.WriteLine("    COLOR: white;")
$txtstream.WriteLine("    BACKGROUND-COLOR: navy;")
$txtstream.WriteLine("    FONT-FAMILY: font-family: Cambria, serif;")
$txtstream.WriteLine("    FONT-SIZE: 12px;")
$txtstream.WriteLine("    text-align: left;")
$txtstream.WriteLine("    display:table-cell;")
$txtstream.WriteLine("    white-Space: nowrap;")
$txtstream.WriteLine("}")
$txtstream.WriteLine("h1 {")
$txtstream.WriteLine("color: antiquewhite;")
$txtstream.WriteLine("text-shadow: 1px 1px 1px black;")
$txtstream.WriteLine("padding: 3px;")
$txtstream.WriteLine("text-align: center;")
$txtstream.WriteLine("box-shadow: invar 2px 2px 5px rgba(0,0,0,0.5), invar -
2px -2px 5px rgba(255,255,255,0.5);")
$txtstream.WriteLine("}")
$txtstream.WriteLine("</style>")
```

OSCILLATING ROW COLORS

```
$txtstream.WriteLine("<style>")
```

```
$txtstream.WriteLine("th")
$txtstream.WriteLine("{")
$txtstream.WriteLine("    COLOR: white;")
$txtstream.WriteLine("    BACKGROUND-COLOR: navy;")
$txtstream.WriteLine("    FONT-FAMILY:font-family: Cambria, serif;")
$txtstream.WriteLine("    FONT-SIZE: 12px;")
$txtstream.WriteLine("    text-align: left;")
$txtstream.WriteLine("    white-Space: nowrap;")
$txtstream.WriteLine("}")
$txtstream.WriteLine("td")
$txtstream.WriteLine("{")
$txtstream.WriteLine("    COLOR: navy;")
$txtstream.WriteLine("    FONT-FAMILY: font-family: Cambria, serif;")
$txtstream.WriteLine("    FONT-SIZE: 12px;")
$txtstream.WriteLine("    text-align: left;")
$txtstream.WriteLine("    white-Space: nowrap;")
$txtstream.WriteLine("}")
$txtstream.WriteLine("div")
$txtstream.WriteLine("{")
$txtstream.WriteLine("    COLOR: navy;")
$txtstream.WriteLine("    FONT-FAMILY: font-family: Cambria, serif;")
$txtstream.WriteLine("    FONT-SIZE: 12px;")
$txtstream.WriteLine("    text-align: left;")
$txtstream.WriteLine("    white-Space: nowrap;")
$txtstream.WriteLine("}")
$txtstream.WriteLine("span")
$txtstream.WriteLine("{")
$txtstream.WriteLine("    COLOR: navy;")
$txtstream.WriteLine("    FONT-FAMILY: font-family: Cambria, serif;")
$txtstream.WriteLine("    FONT-SIZE: 12px;")
$txtstream.WriteLine("    text-align: left;")
$txtstream.WriteLine("    white-Space: nowrap;")
$txtstream.WriteLine("    width: 100%;")
$txtstream.WriteLine("}")
$txtstream.WriteLine("textarea")
$txtstream.WriteLine("{")
$txtstream.WriteLine("    COLOR: navy;")
$txtstream.WriteLine("    FONT-FAMILY: font-family: Cambria, serif;")
$txtstream.WriteLine("    FONT-SIZE: 12px;")
$txtstream.WriteLine("    text-align: left;")
```

```
$txtstream.WriteLine("    white-Space: nowrap;")
$txtstream.WriteLine("    display:inline-block;")
$txtstream.WriteLine("    width: 100%;")
$txtstream.WriteLine("}")
$txtstream.WriteLine("select")
$txtstream.WriteLine("{")
$txtstream.WriteLine("    COLOR: navy;")
$txtstream.WriteLine("    FONT-FAMILY: font-family: Cambria, serif;")
$txtstream.WriteLine("    FONT-SIZE: 10px;")
$txtstream.WriteLine("    text-align: left;")
$txtstream.WriteLine("    white-Space: nowrap;")
$txtstream.WriteLine("    display:inline-block;")
$txtstream.WriteLine("    width: 100%;")
$txtstream.WriteLine("}")
$txtstream.WriteLine("input")
$txtstream.WriteLine("{")
$txtstream.WriteLine("    COLOR: navy;")
$txtstream.WriteLine("    FONT-FAMILY: font-family: Cambria, serif;")
$txtstream.WriteLine("    FONT-SIZE: 12px;")
$txtstream.WriteLine("    text-align: left;")
$txtstream.WriteLine("    display:table-cell;")
$txtstream.WriteLine("    white-Space: nowrap;")
$txtstream.WriteLine("}")
$txtstream.WriteLine("h1 {")
$txtstream.WriteLine("color: antiquewhite;")
$txtstream.WriteLine("text-shadow: 1px 1px 1px black;")
$txtstream.WriteLine("padding: 3px;")
$txtstream.WriteLine("text-align: center;")
$txtstream.WriteLine("box-shadow: invar 2px 2px 5px rgba(0,0,0,0.5), invar -2px -2px 5px rgba(255,255,255,0.5);")
$txtstream.WriteLine("}")
$txtstream.WriteLine("tr:nth-child(even){background-color:#f2f2f2;}")
$txtstream.WriteLine("tr:nth-child(odd){background-color:#cccccc; color:#f2f2f2;}")
$txtstream.WriteLine("</style>")
```

GHOST DECORATED

```
$txtstream.WriteLine("<style type='text/css'>")
$txtstream.WriteLine("th")
```

```
$txtstream.WriteLine("{")
$txtstream.WriteLine("    COLOR: black;")
$txtstream.WriteLine("    BACKGROUND-COLOR: white;")
$txtstream.WriteLine("    FONT-FAMILY:font-family: Cambria, serif;")
$txtstream.WriteLine("    FONT-SIZE: 12px;")
$txtstream.WriteLine("    text-align: left;")
$txtstream.WriteLine("    white-Space: nowrap;")
$txtstream.WriteLine("}")
$txtstream.WriteLine("td")
$txtstream.WriteLine("{")
$txtstream.WriteLine("    COLOR: black;")
$txtstream.WriteLine("    BACKGROUND-COLOR: white;")
$txtstream.WriteLine("    FONT-FAMILY: font-family: Cambria, serif;")
$txtstream.WriteLine("    FONT-SIZE: 12px;")
$txtstream.WriteLine("    text-align: left;")
$txtstream.WriteLine("    white-Space: nowrap;")
$txtstream.WriteLine("}")
$txtstream.WriteLine("div")
$txtstream.WriteLine("{")
$txtstream.WriteLine("    COLOR: black;")
$txtstream.WriteLine("    BACKGROUND-COLOR: white;")
$txtstream.WriteLine("    FONT-FAMILY: font-family: Cambria, serif;")
$txtstream.WriteLine("    FONT-SIZE: 10px;")
$txtstream.WriteLine("    text-align: left;")
$txtstream.WriteLine("    white-Space: nowrap;")
$txtstream.WriteLine("}")
$txtstream.WriteLine("span")
$txtstream.WriteLine("{")
$txtstream.WriteLine("    COLOR: black;")
$txtstream.WriteLine("    BACKGROUND-COLOR: white;")
$txtstream.WriteLine("    FONT-FAMILY: font-family: Cambria, serif;")
$txtstream.WriteLine("    FONT-SIZE: 10px;")
$txtstream.WriteLine("    text-align: left;")
$txtstream.WriteLine("    white-Space: nowrap;")
$txtstream.WriteLine("    display:inline-block;")
$txtstream.WriteLine("    width: 100%;")
$txtstream.WriteLine("}")
$txtstream.WriteLine("textarea")
$txtstream.WriteLine("{")
$txtstream.WriteLine("    COLOR: black;")
```

```
$txtstream.WriteLine("    BACKGROUND-COLOR: white;")
$txtstream.WriteLine("    FONT-FAMILY: font-family: Cambria, serif;")
$txtstream.WriteLine("    FONT-SIZE: 10px;")
$txtstream.WriteLine("    text-align: left;")
$txtstream.WriteLine("    white-Space: nowrap;")
$txtstream.WriteLine("    width: 100%;")
$txtstream.WriteLine("}")
$txtstream.WriteLine("select")
$txtstream.WriteLine("{")
$txtstream.WriteLine("    COLOR: black;")
$txtstream.WriteLine("    BACKGROUND-COLOR: white;")
$txtstream.WriteLine("    FONT-FAMILY: font-family: Cambria, serif;")
$txtstream.WriteLine("    FONT-SIZE: 10px;")
$txtstream.WriteLine("    text-align: left;")
$txtstream.WriteLine("    white-Space: nowrap;")
$txtstream.WriteLine("    width: 100%;")
$txtstream.WriteLine("}")
$txtstream.WriteLine("input")
$txtstream.WriteLine("{")
$txtstream.WriteLine("    COLOR: black;")
$txtstream.WriteLine("    BACKGROUND-COLOR: white;")
$txtstream.WriteLine("    FONT-FAMILY: font-family: Cambria, serif;")
$txtstream.WriteLine("    FONT-SIZE: 12px;")
$txtstream.WriteLine("    text-align: left;")
$txtstream.WriteLine("    display:table-cell;")
$txtstream.WriteLine("    white-Space: nowrap;")
$txtstream.WriteLine("}")
$txtstream.WriteLine("h1 {")
$txtstream.WriteLine("color: antiquewhite;")
$txtstream.WriteLine("text-shadow: 1px 1px 1px black;")
$txtstream.WriteLine("padding: 3px;")
$txtstream.WriteLine("text-align: center;")
$txtstream.WriteLine("box-shadow: invar 2px 2px 5px rgba(0,0,0,0.5), invar -
2px -2px 5px rgba(255,255,255,0.5);")
$txtstream.WriteLine("}")
$txtstream.WriteLine("</style>")
```

```
$txtstream.WriteLine("<style type='text/css'>")
$txtstream.WriteLine("body")
$txtstream.WriteLine("{")
$txtstream.WriteLine("   PADDING-RIGHT: 0px;")
$txtstream.WriteLine("   PADDING-LEFT: 0px;")
$txtstream.WriteLine("   PADDING-BOTTOM: 0px;")
$txtstream.WriteLine("   MARGIN: 0px;")
$txtstream.WriteLine("   COLOR: #333;")
$txtstream.WriteLine("   PADDING-TOP: 0px;")
$txtstream.WriteLine("   FONT-FAMILY: verdana, arial, helvetica, sans-serif;")
$txtstream.WriteLine("}")
$txtstream.WriteLine("table")
$txtstream.WriteLine("{")
$txtstream.WriteLine("   BORDER-RIGHT: #999999 3px solid;")
$txtstream.WriteLine("   PADDING-RIGHT: 6px;")
$txtstream.WriteLine("   PADDING-LEFT: 6px;")
$txtstream.WriteLine("   FONT-WEIGHT: Bold;")
$txtstream.WriteLine("   FONT-SIZE: 14px;")
$txtstream.WriteLine("   PADDING-BOTTOM: 6px;")
$txtstream.WriteLine("   COLOR: Peru;")
$txtstream.WriteLine("   LINE-HEIGHT: 14px;")
$txtstream.WriteLine("   PADDING-TOP: 6px;")
$txtstream.WriteLine("   BORDER-BOTTOM: #999 1px solid;")
$txtstream.WriteLine("   BACKGROUND-COLOR: #eeeeee;")
$txtstream.WriteLine("   FONT-FAMILY: verdana, arial, helvetica, sans-serif;")
$txtstream.WriteLine("   FONT-SIZE: 12px;")
$txtstream.WriteLine("}")
$txtstream.WriteLine("th")
$txtstream.WriteLine("{")
$txtstream.WriteLine("   BORDER-RIGHT: #999999 3px solid;")
$txtstream.WriteLine("   PADDING-RIGHT: 6px;")
$txtstream.WriteLine("   PADDING-LEFT: 6px;")
$txtstream.WriteLine("   FONT-WEIGHT: Bold;")
$txtstream.WriteLine("   FONT-SIZE: 14px;")
$txtstream.WriteLine("   PADDING-BOTTOM: 6px;")
$txtstream.WriteLine("   COLOR: darkred;")
$txtstream.WriteLine("   LINE-HEIGHT: 14px;")
$txtstream.WriteLine("   PADDING-TOP: 6px;")
$txtstream.WriteLine("   BORDER-BOTTOM: #999 1px solid;")
$txtstream.WriteLine("   BACKGROUND-COLOR: #eeeeee;")
```

```
$txtstream.WriteLine("   FONT-FAMILY:font-family: Cambria, serif;")
$txtstream.WriteLine("   FONT-SIZE: 12px;")
$txtstream.WriteLine("   text-align: left;")
$txtstream.WriteLine("   white-Space: nowrap;")
$txtstream.WriteLine("}")
$txtstream.WriteLine(".th")
$txtstream.WriteLine("{")
$txtstream.WriteLine("   BORDER-RIGHT: #999999 2px solid;")
$txtstream.WriteLine("   PADDING-RIGHT: 6px;")
$txtstream.WriteLine("   PADDING-LEFT: 6px;")
$txtstream.WriteLine("   FONT-WEIGHT: Bold;")
$txtstream.WriteLine("   PADDING-BOTTOM: 6px;")
$txtstream.WriteLine("   COLOR: black;")
$txtstream.WriteLine("   PADDING-TOP: 6px;")
$txtstream.WriteLine("   BORDER-BOTTOM: #999 2px solid;")
$txtstream.WriteLine("   BACKGROUND-COLOR: #eeeeee;")
$txtstream.WriteLine("   FONT-FAMILY: font-family: Cambria, serif;")
$txtstream.WriteLine("   FONT-SIZE: 10px;")
$txtstream.WriteLine("   text-align: right;")
$txtstream.WriteLine("   white-Space: nowrap;")
$txtstream.WriteLine("}")
$txtstream.WriteLine("td")
$txtstream.WriteLine("{")
$txtstream.WriteLine("   BORDER-RIGHT: #999999 3px solid;")
$txtstream.WriteLine("   PADDING-RIGHT: 6px;")
$txtstream.WriteLine("   PADDING-LEFT: 6px;")
$txtstream.WriteLine("   FONT-WEIGHT: Normal;")
$txtstream.WriteLine("   PADDING-BOTTOM: 6px;")
$txtstream.WriteLine("   COLOR: navy;")
$txtstream.WriteLine("   LINE-HEIGHT: 14px;")
$txtstream.WriteLine("   PADDING-TOP: 6px;")
$txtstream.WriteLine("   BORDER-BOTTOM: #999 1px solid;")
$txtstream.WriteLine("   BACKGROUND-COLOR: #eeeeee;")
$txtstream.WriteLine("   FONT-FAMILY: font-family: Cambria, serif;")
$txtstream.WriteLine("   FONT-SIZE: 12px;")
$txtstream.WriteLine("   text-align: left;")
$txtstream.WriteLine("   white-Space: nowrap;")
$txtstream.WriteLine("}")
$txtstream.WriteLine("div")
$txtstream.WriteLine("{")
```

```
$txtstream.WriteLine("    BORDER-RIGHT: #999999 3px solid;")
$txtstream.WriteLine("    PADDING-RIGHT: 6px;")
$txtstream.WriteLine("    PADDING-LEFT: 6px;")
$txtstream.WriteLine("    FONT-WEIGHT: Normal;")
$txtstream.WriteLine("    PADDING-BOTTOM: 6px;")
$txtstream.WriteLine("    COLOR: white;")
$txtstream.WriteLine("    PADDING-TOP: 6px;")
$txtstream.WriteLine("    BORDER-BOTTOM: #999 1px solid;")
$txtstream.WriteLine("    BACKGROUND-COLOR: navy;")
$txtstream.WriteLine("    FONT-FAMILY: font-family: Cambria, serif;")
$txtstream.WriteLine("    FONT-SIZE: 10px;")
$txtstream.WriteLine("    text-align: left;")
$txtstream.WriteLine("    white-Space: nowrap;")
$txtstream.WriteLine("}")
$txtstream.WriteLine("span")
$txtstream.WriteLine("{")
$txtstream.WriteLine("    BORDER-RIGHT: #999999 3px solid;")
$txtstream.WriteLine("    PADDING-RIGHT: 3px;")
$txtstream.WriteLine("    PADDING-LEFT: 3px;")
$txtstream.WriteLine("    FONT-WEIGHT: Normal;")
$txtstream.WriteLine("    PADDING-BOTTOM: 3px;")
$txtstream.WriteLine("    COLOR: white;")
$txtstream.WriteLine("    PADDING-TOP: 3px;")
$txtstream.WriteLine("    BORDER-BOTTOM: #999 1px solid;")
$txtstream.WriteLine("    BACKGROUND-COLOR: navy;")
$txtstream.WriteLine("    FONT-FAMILY: font-family: Cambria, serif;")
$txtstream.WriteLine("    FONT-SIZE: 10px;")
$txtstream.WriteLine("    text-align: left;")
$txtstream.WriteLine("    white-Space: nowrap;")
$txtstream.WriteLine("    display:inline-block;")
$txtstream.WriteLine("    width: 100%;")
$txtstream.WriteLine("}")
$txtstream.WriteLine("textarea")
$txtstream.WriteLine("{")
$txtstream.WriteLine("    BORDER-RIGHT: #999999 3px solid;")
$txtstream.WriteLine("    PADDING-RIGHT: 3px;")
$txtstream.WriteLine("    PADDING-LEFT: 3px;")
$txtstream.WriteLine("    FONT-WEIGHT: Normal;")
$txtstream.WriteLine("    PADDING-BOTTOM: 3px;")
$txtstream.WriteLine("    COLOR: white;")
```

```
$txtstream.WriteLine("    PADDING-TOP: 3px;")
$txtstream.WriteLine("    BORDER-BOTTOM: #999 1px solid;")
$txtstream.WriteLine("    BACKGROUND-COLOR: navy;")
$txtstream.WriteLine("    FONT-FAMILY: font-family: Cambria, serif;")
$txtstream.WriteLine("    FONT-SIZE: 10px;")
$txtstream.WriteLine("    text-align: left;")
$txtstream.WriteLine("    white-Space: nowrap;")
$txtstream.WriteLine("    width: 100%;")
$txtstream.WriteLine("}")
$txtstream.WriteLine("select")
$txtstream.WriteLine("{")
$txtstream.WriteLine("    BORDER-RIGHT: #999999 3px solid;")
$txtstream.WriteLine("    PADDING-RIGHT: 6px;")
$txtstream.WriteLine("    PADDING-LEFT: 6px;")
$txtstream.WriteLine("    FONT-WEIGHT: Normal;")
$txtstream.WriteLine("    PADDING-BOTTOM: 6px;")
$txtstream.WriteLine("    COLOR: white;")
$txtstream.WriteLine("    PADDING-TOP: 6px;")
$txtstream.WriteLine("    BORDER-BOTTOM: #999 1px solid;")
$txtstream.WriteLine("    BACKGROUND-COLOR: navy;")
$txtstream.WriteLine("    FONT-FAMILY: font-family: Cambria, serif;")
$txtstream.WriteLine("    FONT-SIZE: 10px;")
$txtstream.WriteLine("    text-align: left;")
$txtstream.WriteLine("    white-Space: nowrap;")
$txtstream.WriteLine("    width: 100%;")
$txtstream.WriteLine("}")
$txtstream.WriteLine("input")
$txtstream.WriteLine("{")
$txtstream.WriteLine("    BORDER-RIGHT: #999999 3px solid;")
$txtstream.WriteLine("    PADDING-RIGHT: 3px;")
$txtstream.WriteLine("    PADDING-LEFT: 3px;")
$txtstream.WriteLine("    FONT-WEIGHT: Bold;")
$txtstream.WriteLine("    PADDING-BOTTOM: 3px;")
$txtstream.WriteLine("    COLOR: white;")
$txtstream.WriteLine("    PADDING-TOP: 3px;")
$txtstream.WriteLine("    BORDER-BOTTOM: #999 1px solid;")
$txtstream.WriteLine("    BACKGROUND-COLOR: navy;")
$txtstream.WriteLine("    FONT-FAMILY: font-family: Cambria, serif;")
$txtstream.WriteLine("    FONT-SIZE: 12px;")
$txtstream.WriteLine("    text-align: left;")
```

```
$txtstream.WriteLine("    display:table-cell;")
$txtstream.WriteLine("    white-Space: nowrap;")
$txtstream.WriteLine("    width: 100%;")
$txtstream.WriteLine("}")
$txtstream.WriteLine("h1 {")
$txtstream.WriteLine("color: antiquewhite;")
$txtstream.WriteLine("text-shadow: 1px 1px black;")
$txtstream.WriteLine("padding: 3px;")
$txtstream.WriteLine("text-align: center;")
$txtstream.WriteLine("box-shadow: invar 2px 5px rgba(0,0,0,0.5), invar -2px -2px 5px rgba(255,255,255,0.5);")
$txtstream.WriteLine("}")
$txtstream.WriteLine("</style>")
```

SHADOW BOX

```
$txtstream.WriteLine("<style type='text/css'>")
$txtstream.WriteLine("body")
$txtstream.WriteLine("{")
$txtstream.WriteLine("    PADDING-RIGHT: 0px;")
$txtstream.WriteLine("    PADDING-LEFT: 0px;")
$txtstream.WriteLine("    PADDING-BOTTOM: 0px;")
$txtstream.WriteLine("    MARGIN: 0px;")
$txtstream.WriteLine("    COLOR: #333;")
$txtstream.WriteLine("    PADDING-TOP: 0px;")
$txtstream.WriteLine("    FONT-FAMILY: verdana, arial, helvetica, sans-serif;")
$txtstream.WriteLine("}")
$txtstream.WriteLine("table")
$txtstream.WriteLine("{")
$txtstream.WriteLine("    BORDER-RIGHT: #999999 1px solid;")
$txtstream.WriteLine("    PADDING-RIGHT: 1px;")
$txtstream.WriteLine("    PADDING-LEFT: 1px;")
$txtstream.WriteLine("    PADDING-BOTTOM: 1px;")
$txtstream.WriteLine("    LINE-HEIGHT: 8px;")
$txtstream.WriteLine("    PADDING-TOP: 1px;")
$txtstream.WriteLine("    BORDER-BOTTOM: #999 1px solid;")
$txtstream.WriteLine("    BACKGROUND-COLOR: #eeeeee;")
$txtstream.WriteLine("    filter:progid:DXImageTransform.Microsoft.Shadow(color='silver',    Direction=135, Strength=16)")
```

```
$txtstream.WriteLine("}")
$txtstream.WriteLine("th")
$txtstream.WriteLine("{")
$txtstream.WriteLine("    BORDER-RIGHT: #999999 3px solid;")
$txtstream.WriteLine("    PADDING-RIGHT: 6px;")
$txtstream.WriteLine("    PADDING-LEFT: 6px;")
$txtstream.WriteLine("    FONT-WEIGHT: Bold;")
$txtstream.WriteLine("    FONT-SIZE: 14px;")
$txtstream.WriteLine("    PADDING-BOTTOM: 6px;")
$txtstream.WriteLine("    COLOR: darkred;")
$txtstream.WriteLine("    LINE-HEIGHT: 14px;")
$txtstream.WriteLine("    PADDING-TOP: 6px;")
$txtstream.WriteLine("    BORDER-BOTTOM: #999 1px solid;")
$txtstream.WriteLine("    BACKGROUND-COLOR: #eeeeee;")
$txtstream.WriteLine("    FONT-FAMILY: font-family: Cambria, serif;")
$txtstream.WriteLine("    FONT-SIZE: 12px;")
$txtstream.WriteLine("    text-align: left;")
$txtstream.WriteLine("    white-Space: nowrap;")
$txtstream.WriteLine("}")
$txtstream.WriteLine(".th")
$txtstream.WriteLine("{")
$txtstream.WriteLine("    BORDER-RIGHT: #999999 2px solid;")
$txtstream.WriteLine("    PADDING-RIGHT: 6px;")
$txtstream.WriteLine("    PADDING-LEFT: 6px;")
$txtstream.WriteLine("    FONT-WEIGHT: Bold;")
$txtstream.WriteLine("    PADDING-BOTTOM: 6px;")
$txtstream.WriteLine("    COLOR: black;")
$txtstream.WriteLine("    PADDING-TOP: 6px;")
$txtstream.WriteLine("    BORDER-BOTTOM: #999 2px solid;")
$txtstream.WriteLine("    BACKGROUND-COLOR: #eeeeee;")
$txtstream.WriteLine("    FONT-FAMILY: font-family: Cambria, serif;")
$txtstream.WriteLine("    FONT-SIZE: 10px;")
$txtstream.WriteLine("    text-align: right;")
$txtstream.WriteLine("    white-Space: nowrap;")
$txtstream.WriteLine("}")
$txtstream.WriteLine("td")
$txtstream.WriteLine("{")
$txtstream.WriteLine("    BORDER-RIGHT: #999999 3px solid;")
$txtstream.WriteLine("    PADDING-RIGHT: 6px;")
$txtstream.WriteLine("    PADDING-LEFT: 6px;")
```

```
$txtstream.WriteLine("    FONT-WEIGHT: Normal;")
$txtstream.WriteLine("    PADDING-BOTTOM: 6px;")
$txtstream.WriteLine("    COLOR: navy;")
$txtstream.WriteLine("    LINE-HEIGHT: 14px;")
$txtstream.WriteLine("    PADDING-TOP: 6px;")
$txtstream.WriteLine("    BORDER-BOTTOM: #999 1px solid;")
$txtstream.WriteLine("    BACKGROUND-COLOR: #eeeeee;")
$txtstream.WriteLine("    FONT-FAMILY: font-family: Cambria, serif;")
$txtstream.WriteLine("    FONT-SIZE: 12px;")
$txtstream.WriteLine("    text-align: left;")
$txtstream.WriteLine("    white-Space: nowrap;")
$txtstream.WriteLine("}")
$txtstream.WriteLine("div")
$txtstream.WriteLine("{")
$txtstream.WriteLine("    BORDER-RIGHT: #999999 3px solid;")
$txtstream.WriteLine("    PADDING-RIGHT: 6px;")
$txtstream.WriteLine("    PADDING-LEFT: 6px;")
$txtstream.WriteLine("    FONT-WEIGHT: Normal;")
$txtstream.WriteLine("    PADDING-BOTTOM: 6px;")
$txtstream.WriteLine("    COLOR: white;")
$txtstream.WriteLine("    PADDING-TOP: 6px;")
$txtstream.WriteLine("    BORDER-BOTTOM: #999 1px solid;")
$txtstream.WriteLine("    BACKGROUND-COLOR: navy;")
$txtstream.WriteLine("    FONT-FAMILY: font-family: Cambria, serif;")
$txtstream.WriteLine("    FONT-SIZE: 10px;")
$txtstream.WriteLine("    text-align: left;")
$txtstream.WriteLine("    white-Space: nowrap;")
$txtstream.WriteLine("}")
$txtstream.WriteLine("span")
$txtstream.WriteLine("{")
$txtstream.WriteLine("    BORDER-RIGHT: #999999 3px solid;")
$txtstream.WriteLine("    PADDING-RIGHT: 3px;")
$txtstream.WriteLine("    PADDING-LEFT: 3px;")
$txtstream.WriteLine("    FONT-WEIGHT: Normal;")
$txtstream.WriteLine("    PADDING-BOTTOM: 3px;")
$txtstream.WriteLine("    COLOR: white;")
$txtstream.WriteLine("    PADDING-TOP: 3px;")
$txtstream.WriteLine("    BORDER-BOTTOM: #999 1px solid;")
$txtstream.WriteLine("    BACKGROUND-COLOR: navy;")
$txtstream.WriteLine("    FONT-FAMILY: font-family: Cambria, serif;")
```

```
$txtstream.WriteLine("   FONT-SIZE: 10px;")
$txtstream.WriteLine("   text-align: left;")
$txtstream.WriteLine("   white-Space: nowrap;")
$txtstream.WriteLine("   display: inline-block;")
$txtstream.WriteLine("   width: 100%;")
$txtstream.WriteLine("}")
$txtstream.WriteLine("textarea")
$txtstream.WriteLine("{")
$txtstream.WriteLine("   BORDER-RIGHT: #999999 3px solid;")
$txtstream.WriteLine("   PADDING-RIGHT: 3px;")
$txtstream.WriteLine("   PADDING-LEFT: 3px;")
$txtstream.WriteLine("   FONT-WEIGHT: Normal;")
$txtstream.WriteLine("   PADDING-BOTTOM: 3px;")
$txtstream.WriteLine("   COLOR: white;")
$txtstream.WriteLine("   PADDING-TOP: 3px;")
$txtstream.WriteLine("   BORDER-BOTTOM: #999 1px solid;")
$txtstream.WriteLine("   BACKGROUND-COLOR: navy;")
$txtstream.WriteLine("   FONT-FAMILY: font-family: Cambria, serif;")
$txtstream.WriteLine("   FONT-SIZE: 10px;")
$txtstream.WriteLine("   text-align: left;")
$txtstream.WriteLine("   white-Space: nowrap;")
$txtstream.WriteLine("   width: 100%;")
$txtstream.WriteLine("}")
$txtstream.WriteLine("select")
$txtstream.WriteLine("{")
$txtstream.WriteLine("   BORDER-RIGHT: #999999 3px solid;")
$txtstream.WriteLine("   PADDING-RIGHT: 6px;")
$txtstream.WriteLine("   PADDING-LEFT: 6px;")
$txtstream.WriteLine("   FONT-WEIGHT: Normal;")
$txtstream.WriteLine("   PADDING-BOTTOM: 6px;")
$txtstream.WriteLine("   COLOR: white;")
$txtstream.WriteLine("   PADDING-TOP: 6px;")
$txtstream.WriteLine("   BORDER-BOTTOM: #999 1px solid;")
$txtstream.WriteLine("   BACKGROUND-COLOR: navy;")
$txtstream.WriteLine("   FONT-FAMILY: font-family: Cambria, serif;")
$txtstream.WriteLine("   FONT-SIZE: 10px;")
$txtstream.WriteLine("   text-align: left;")
$txtstream.WriteLine("   white-Space: nowrap;")
$txtstream.WriteLine("   width: 100%;")
$txtstream.WriteLine("}")
```

```
$txtstream.WriteLine("input")
$txtstream.WriteLine("{")
$txtstream.WriteLine("    BORDER-RIGHT: #999999 3px solid;")
$txtstream.WriteLine("    PADDING-RIGHT: 3px;")
$txtstream.WriteLine("    PADDING-LEFT: 3px;")
$txtstream.WriteLine("    FONT-WEIGHT: Bold;")
$txtstream.WriteLine("    PADDING-BOTTOM: 3px;")
$txtstream.WriteLine("    COLOR: white;")
$txtstream.WriteLine("    PADDING-TOP: 3px;")
$txtstream.WriteLine("    BORDER-BOTTOM: #999 1px solid;")
$txtstream.WriteLine("    BACKGROUND-COLOR: navy;")
$txtstream.WriteLine("    FONT-FAMILY: font-family: Cambria, serif;")
$txtstream.WriteLine("    FONT-SIZE: 12px;")
$txtstream.WriteLine("    text-align: left;")
$txtstream.WriteLine("    display: table-cell;")
$txtstream.WriteLine("    white-Space: nowrap;")
$txtstream.WriteLine("    width: 100%;")
$txtstream.WriteLine("}")
$txtstream.WriteLine("h1 {")
$txtstream.WriteLine("color: antiquewhite;")
$txtstream.WriteLine("text-shadow: 1px 1px 1px black;")
$txtstream.WriteLine("padding: 3px;")
$txtstream.WriteLine("text-align: center;")
$txtstream.WriteLine("box-shadow: invar 2px 2px 5px rgba(0,0,0,0.5), invar -
2px -2px 5px rgba(255,255,255,0.5);")
$txtstream.WriteLine("}")
$txtstream.WriteLine("</style>")
```

Appendix B
List of Locales

elow, is A list of locales you can use with your PowerShell Connections. You only need one, obviously, and that will the one for your country.

Name	Locale Code
Afrikaans - South Africa	MS_0436
Albanian - Albania	MS_041c
Alsatian	MS_0484
Amharic - Ethiopia	MS_045e
Arabic - Saudi Arabia	MS_0401
Arabic - Algeria	MS_1401
Arabic - Bahrain	MS_3c01
Arabic - Egypt	MS_0c01
Arabic - Iraq	MS_0801
Arabic - Jordan	MS_2c01
Arabic - Kuwait	MS_3401
Arabic - Lebanon	MS_3001
Arabic - Libya	MS_1001
Arabic - Morocco	MS_1801
Arabic - Oman	MS_2001
Arabic - Qatar	MS_4001
Arabic - Syria	MS_2801
Arabic - Tunisia	MS_1c01
Arabic - U.A.E.	MS_3801
Arabic - Yemen	MS_2401

Armenian - Armenia	MS_042b
Assamese	MS_044d
Azeri (Cyrillic)	MS_082c
Azeri (Latin)	MS_042c
Bashkir	MS_046d
Basque	MS_042d
Belarusian	MS_0423
Bengali (India)	MS_0445
Bengali (Bangladesh)	MS_0845
Bosnian (Bosnia/Herzegovina)	MS_141A
Breton	MS_047e
Bulgarian	MS_0402
Burmese	MS_0455
Catalan	MS_0403
Cherokee - United States	MS_045c
Chinese - People's Republic of China	MS_0804
Chinese - Singapore	MS_1004
Chinese - Taiwan	MS_0404
Chinese - Hong Kong SAR	MS_0c04
Chinese - Macao SAR	MS_1404
Corsican	MS_0483
Croatian	MS_041a
Croatian (Bosnia/Herzegovina)	MS_101a
Czech	MS_0405
Danish	MS_0406
Dari	MS_048c
Divehi	MS_0465
Dutch - Netherlands	MS_0413
Dutch - Belgium	MS_0813
Edo	MS_0466
English - United States	MS_0409
English - United Kingdom	MS_0809
English - Australia	MS_0c09
English - Belize	MS_2809
English - Canada	MS_1009
English - Caribbean	MS_2409
English - Hong Kong SAR	MS_3c09
English - India	MS_4009
English - Indonesia	MS_3809
English - Ireland	MS_1809
English - Jamaica	MS_2009
English - Malaysia	MS_4409
English - New Zealand	MS_1409
English - Philippines	MS_3409

English - Singapore	MS_4809
English - South Africa	MS_1c09
English - Trinidad	MS_2c09
English - Zimbabwe	MS_3009
Estonian	MS_0425
Faroese	MS_0438
Farsi	MS_0429
Filipino	MS_0464
Finnish	MS_040b
French - France	MS_040c
French - Belgium	MS_080c
French - Cameroon	MS_2c0c
French - Canada	MS_0c0c
French - Democratic Rep. of Congo	MS_240c
French - Cote d'Ivoire	MS_300c
French - Haiti	MS_3c0c
French - Luxembourg	MS_140c
French - Mali	MS_340c
French - Monaco	MS_180c
French - Morocco	MS_380c
French - North Africa	MS_e40c
French - Reunion	MS_200c
French - Senegal	MS_280c
French - Switzerland	MS_100c
French - West Indies	MS_1c0c
Frisian - Netherlands	MS_0462
Fulfulde - Nigeria	MS_0467
FYRO Macedonian	MS_042f
Galician	MS_0456
Georgian	MS_0437
German - Germany	MS_0407
German - Austria	MS_0c07
German - Liechtenstein	MS_1407
German - Luxembourg	MS_1007
German - Switzerland	MS_0807
Greek	MS_0408
Greenlandic	MS_046f
Guarani - Paraguay	MS_0474
Gujarati	MS_0447
Hausa - Nigeria	MS_0468
Hawaiian - United States	MS_0475
Hebrew	MS_040d
Hindi	MS_0439
Hungarian	MS_040e

Ibibio - Nigeria	MS_0469
Icelandic	MS_040f
Igbo - Nigeria	MS_0470
Indonesian	MS_0421
Inuktitut	MS_045d
Irish	MS_083c
Italian - Italy	MS_0410
Italian - Switzerland	MS_0810
Japanese	MS_0411
K'iche	MS_0486
Kannada	MS_044b
Kanuri - Nigeria	MS_0471
Kashmiri	MS_0860
Kashmiri (Arabic)	MS_0460
Kazakh	MS_043f
Khmer	MS_0453
Kinyarwanda	MS_0487
Konkani	MS_0457
Korean	MS_0412
Kyrgyz (Cyrillic)	MS_0440
Lao	MS_0454
Latin	MS_0476
Latvian	MS_0426
Lithuanian	MS_0427
Luxembourgish	MS_046e
Malay - Malaysia	MS_043e
Malay - Brunei Darussalam	MS_083e
Malayalam	MS_044c
Maltese	MS_043a
Manipuri	MS_0458
Maori - New Zealand	MS_0481
Mapudungun	MS_0471
Marathi	MS_044e
Mohawk	MS_047c
Mongolian (Cyrillic)	MS_0450
Mongolian (Mongolian)	MS_0850
Nepali	MS_0461
Nepali - India	MS_0861
Norwegian (Bokmål)	MS_0414
Norwegian (Nynorsk)	MS_0814
Occitan	MS_0482
Oriya	MS_0448
Oromo	MS_0472
Papiamentu	MS_0479

Pashto	MS_0463
Polish	MS_0415
Portuguese - Brazil	MS_0416
Portuguese - Portugal	MS_0816
Punjabi	MS_0446
Punjabi (Pakistan)	MS_0846
Quecha - Bolivia	MS_046B
Quecha - Ecuador	MS_086B
Quecha - Peru	MS_0C6B
Rhaeto-Romanic	MS_0417
Romanian	MS_0418
Romanian - Moldava	MS_0818
Russian	MS_0419
Russian - Moldava	MS_0819
Sami (Lappish)	MS_043b
Sanskrit	MS_044f
Scottish Gaelic	MS_043c
Sepedi	MS_046c
Serbian (Cyrillic)	MS_0c1a
Serbian (Latin)	MS_081a
Sindhi - India	MS_0459
Sindhi - Pakistan	MS_0859
Sinhalese - Sri Lanka	MS_045b
Slovak	MS_041b
Slovenian	MS_0424
Somali	MS_0477
Sorbian	MS_042e
Spanish - Spain (Modern Sort)	MS_0c0a
Spanish - Spain (Traditional Sort)	MS_040a
Spanish - Argentina	MS_2c0a
Spanish - Bolivia	MS_400a
Spanish - Chile	MS_340a
Spanish - Colombia	MS_240a
Spanish - Costa Rica	MS_140a
Spanish - Dominican Republic	MS_1c0a
Spanish - Ecuador	MS_300a
Spanish - El Salvador	MS_440a
Spanish - Guatemala	MS_100a
Spanish - Honduras	MS_480a
Spanish - Latin America	MS_580a
Spanish - Mexico	MS_080a
Spanish - Nicaragua	MS_4c0a
Spanish - Panama	MS_180a
Spanish - Paraguay	MS_3c0a

Spanish - Peru	MS_280a
Spanish - Puerto Rico	MS_500a
Spanish - United States	MS_540a
Spanish - Uruguay	MS_380a
Spanish - Venezuela	MS_200a
Sutu	MS_0430
Swahili	MS_0441
Swedish	MS_041d
Swedish - Finland	MS_081d
Syriac	MS_045a
Tajik	MS_0428
Tamazight (Arabic)	MS_045f
Tamazight (Latin)	MS_085f
Tamil	MS_0449
Tatar	MS_0444
Telugu	MS_044a
Thai	MS_041e
Tibetan - Bhutan	MS_0851
Tibetan - People's Republic of China	MS_0451
Tigrigna - Eritrea	MS_0873
Tigrigna - Ethiopia	MS_0473
Tsonga	MS_0431
Tswana	MS_0432
Turkish	MS_041f
Turkmen	MS_0442
Uighur - China	MS_0480
Ukrainian	MS_0422
Urdu	MS_0420
Urdu - India	MS_0820
Uzbek (Cyrillic)	MS_0843
Uzbek (Latin)	MS_0443
Venda	MS_0433
Vietnamese	MS_042a
Welsh	MS_0452
Wolof	MS_0488
Xhosa	MS_0434
Yakut	MS_0485
Yi	MS_0478
Yiddish	MS_043d
Yoruba	MS_046a
Zulu	MS_0435
HID (Human Interface Device)	MS_04ff